Blessed Relief

What *Christians* Can Learn
from *Buddhists*
about Suffering

Gordon Peerman

Walking Toget...

SKYLIG...
PUBLISHING
Woodstock, Vermont

Blessed Relief:
What Christians Can Learn from Buddhists about Suffering
2014 Quality Paperback Edition, Third Printing

Library of Congress Cataloging-in-Publication Data
Peerman, Gordon, 1951–
Blessed relief : what Christians can learn from Buddhists about suffering / Gordon Peerman.
p. cm.
Includes bibliographical references.
ISBN-13: 978-1-59473-252-2 (pbk.)
ISBN-10: 1-59473-252-3 (pbk.)
1. Buddhism—Relations—Christianity. 2. Christianity and other religions— Buddhism. 3. Suffering—Religious aspects—Buddhism. I. Title.
BR128.B8P44 2008
294.3'4442—dc22

2008023594

ISBN 978-1-59473-419-9 (eBook)

10 9 8 7 6 5 4 3
Manufactured in the United States of America
Cover Design: Jenny Buono

SkyLight Paths is creating a place where people of different spiritual traditions come together for challenge and inspiration, a place where we can help each other understand the mystery that lies at the heart of our existence.

SkyLight Paths sees both believers and seekers as a community that increasingly transcends traditional boundaries of religion and denomination—people wanting to learn from each other, *walking together, finding the way.*

SkyLight Paths, "Walking Together, Finding the Way" and colophon are trademarks of LongHill Partners, Inc., registered in the U.S. Patent and Trademark Office.

Walking Together, Finding the Way®
Published by SkyLight Paths Publishing
A Division of LongHill Partners, Inc.
Sunset Farm Offices, Route 4, P.O. Box 237
Woodstock, VT 05091
Tel: (802) 457-4000 Fax: (802) 457-4004
www.skylightpaths.com

For Alex and Kathy

and for

C. Gordon Peerman Jr., MD, my father
(1926–2006)

and

John S. Johnson, MD, my friend
(1936–2007)

Contents

Introduction

The Buddha Way and the Christian Way

It was the end of a monthlong silent retreat at Spirit Rock Meditation Center in northern California, and I was looking for a way to the Oakland airport. A man whose practice I had admired over the course of the retreat made eye contact, signaling that he'd give me a ride. I had noticed his careful concentration during our periods of walking meditation. We both did our walking meditation outside in the woods, and he was dependably there, whatever the weather. It seemed odd to me that one day he disappeared from the retreat and was gone for a time, only to return for the final week. It turned out that his father had died, and he had gone home for the funeral. After a week at home with his family, he had come back to sit in the silence and stillness of the last week of the retreat. All this I would learn on the ride to the airport.

The man's name was Kurt Hoelting, and among other things, Kurt was a commercial fisherman, having fished the waters of Alaska since the summers of his college years. He had worked as a Congregational minister until fishing in Alaska called more powerfully to him than college chaplaincy. He had come to Zen by way of the Christian contemplative prayer he'd done with the Trappists. Ever since his first encounter with his

Zen teacher, Robert Aitken Roshi, at a Trappist monastery, Kurt had found himself drawn ever more deeply into Buddhist practice.

Like Kurt, I had come to Buddhist practice by way of Thomas Merton and the Trappists. I have been an Episcopal priest for thirty years and, for at least the last twenty-five, have been moving toward a hyphenated Buddhist-Christian spiritual identity. At home in both traditions, with a kind of dual citizenship, I slip back and forth across the border between the two.

Long before images of the Buddha in human form were ever fashioned, the Buddhist way was depicted simply as a pair of footprints. Very *big* footprints. Jesus, the Buddha, Moses and the Prophets, Muhammad, Lao Tzu—all set out on journeys and left big footprints along the way. Jesus's path—his life, death, and resurrection—are, as I see it, particular footprints along a universal path.

My own path has led through centering prayer to Zen practice, to the homecoming I've found in insight meditation, or *vipassana*. Like many Christians exploring Buddhist ways, I've been helped by a variety of Western and Asian teachers across the Buddhist spectrum: Theravada, Mahayana, and Vajrayana. I find myself bringing what I have discovered in the riches of these traditions back to my birthright Christian community. In my church, I'm known as the Buddhist priest. In the Buddhist *sangha*, I'm known as the Christian priest. From the encounter within myself between Buddhism and Christianity, a synthesis, a dual religious identity, has taken birth. I no longer have the sense that I have to be one or the other, Buddhist or Christian, exclusively in either setting.

Today when I preach in Christian churches, I feel free to use Buddhist and Christian sources to point to the way of Jesus and the freedom of the gospel. The English Buddhist teacher Christmas Humphreys once said that he didn't need to give up the gospel to read Hui Neng (the Sixth Zen Patriarch). And I don't need to give up Thich Nhat Hanh to read Matthew, Mark, Luke, and John.

What Helps and What Doesn't

As a psychotherapist, I'm always on the lookout for what helps people who are suffering, and Buddhist teachers know a lot about suffering—what helps and what doesn't. Buddhists have accumulated 2,500 years of wisdom about how human beings can work with the many varieties of suffering in their lives. Buddhist teachers also know a lot about cultivating happiness, generosity, kindness, and equanimity. It is this combination of deep wisdom in addressing suffering and profound, lighthearted insight about what leads to genuine happiness that has made the Buddhist path so compelling for me.

As a student of contemplative practices, I am also interested in the foundational stories that different faith communities tell and how they relate to people's personal stories. Christian proclamation tells the story of Jesus, and the church invites people to make links between that story and their personal stories. At its best, a Christian community can become a refuge where you can "tell your story." In such a refuge, telling your story and reading it in light of a larger story can help make meaning and sense of what is confusing, frightening, or unbearable. While scripture means different things to different people and is interpreted in a variety of ways, it is first a collection of stories of encounters with God. How those stories are read, which stories come to be held as the most important, and what those stories mean, all occasion differing interpretations and considerable controversy and conflict in Christian circles. Christian communities are both held together and split apart by the different ways the larger story is read.

Buddhists also tell stories—stories about the Buddha, about their teachers, about meditative practice. The Buddhist teachers I've sat with are master storytellers. However, much of Buddhist group practice is done in silence, and there is comparatively little space for telling one's own story, especially in silent retreat settings. In contrast to Christian churches, at least in the emerging Western Buddhism, the emphasis is less on "telling your story" than on what is called "dropping your story line."

Dropping Your Story Line

"Dropping your story line" is, first, a way to notice the suffering that comes with attachment to your story about what has happened and what is going to happen. Then, through what Buddhists call "skillful means," it is possible to learn how to drop your story line about the past and the future, to let go of the constricting identity of yourself as "the sufferer," and to come into the freedom of the present moment. Through dropping the story line you may discover a surprising freedom. As one Buddhist teacher put it, "We take things very personally. The more tightly we hold self, the more problem. No self, well … (laughing) … no problem!" Though Buddhist communities have their problems, because they have contemplative methods for observing and releasing the suffering that comes with certain stories, they have much to teach Christian communities about how to metabolize both personal and communal conflict.

Both telling your story and dropping your story line have an appropriate place in helping people who are suffering. There are promise and peril in both. I remember vividly when one person told me her story of suddenly coming upon the dead body of a colleague. Well-meaning people attempted to reassure or distract her from the horror of her experience; they would prematurely try to get her to drop her story. She wasn't at all ready to do that, and she was grateful that I would hear her out.

Yet we can become stuck in our stories, rehearsing the litanies of disappointment or loss or betrayal, to no good effect.

Rather than helping us work through our suffering, these recitals can dig us deeper into suffering's hole. Dropping the story line is one way to stop digging. In an account of his experience with cancer, *A Whole New Life*, novelist Reynolds Price wrote that, upon being told he had a cancer of the spine that would leave him paralyzed, the kindest thing anyone could have said to him at the moment was, "You're dead. Who are you going to be tomorrow?" Price knew that his old life, his story as he had formerly told it, was over and that what was to come was unknown. When we drop the story line, there follows a shift, a stepping beyond the confines of the ego and all its fears. This is a step into freedom.

In his own day, the Buddha stepped into freedom. Over the course of his forty-five years of teaching, the Buddha said he had but one thing to teach: suffering and the end of suffering. His teaching was a generous offering of skillful means for both seeing suffering directly and ending suffering.

Finding Freedom

On our ride to the Oakland airport, Kurt Hoelting and I discovered that we shared many similar experiences. Both of us had been ordained in Christian churches, both of us had found ourselves drawn to the Buddhist path, and both of us greatly valued the contemplative retreat experiences, Christian and Buddhist, that had shaped us. Kurt told me that he led contemplative kayaking retreats for environmentalists and Jewish rabbis, and he wondered if I would be interested in joining him to lead such a wilderness retreat for Christian clergy in the Inside Passage of southeast Alaska.

I did so in the summer of 2006, and it was that journey that gave birth to the idea for this book. The title of our trip was "From Fear to Freedom." Once we were launched together into the wild, the trip participants told us that it was not only the chance to kayak in Alaska but also the opportunity to practice moving from fear to freedom that had hooked them. Our journey took place within the Tebenkof Bay Wilderness of southeast Alaska, where we could experience wilderness exploration on a deeper level by including the equally vast and powerful resources of the contemplative mind.

Once in Alaska, at night around the campfire, we began to name some of the fears we had brought with us—and others we had discovered once there. The stories we told, our personal stories and how they intersected with the big stories and big footprints along the way, were set within the magnificent Alaskan landscape and soundscape. The sounds of raven, bald eagle, and humpback whale punctuated our talk. As honesty deepened in the silence, we acknowledged all sorts of fears. And we found freedom both in the shared disclosure and in the deep, quiet stillness underneath those fears.

Blessed Relief is a book about dropping fear and all its companion stories and finding your freedom. Throughout the book, I've used the thread of my retreat experiences to link these themes of dropping fear and finding freedom. The silence and hospitality of Benedictine and Trappist communities, along with the kindness and interest in sharing the dharma every Buddhist *sangha* has offered this Christian priest, have been gifts of grace. From my very first retreat with Henri Nouwen while a student at Yale Divinity School, retreats have laid down a path for me to follow the way to freedom.

From retreat experience, from working with participants in my mindfulness-based stress reduction classes, and from doing psychotherapy over two decades, I have collected nine Buddhist practices that can bring blessed relief to a wide range of human suffering. At the end of each chapter of this book, you will find instruction in a particular practice. These practices are invitations for you to make your own journey into freedom. It is one thing to read a book about finding relief from suffering; it is altogether another to *try for yourself* these practices as a way to address your own suffering. You may find that a particular practice speaks to you. Try it. See for yourself. When you find your own "blessed relief," you may discover, like so many others, that these practices, in time, become a way of life, a way to let go of suffering, a way to freedom.

1

BIG MIND, BIG MEDICINE

*Try to be mindful, and let things take their natural course.
Then your mind will become still in any surroundings, like a
clear forest pool. All kinds of wonderful, rare animals will
come to drink at the pool, and you will clearly see the nature of
all things. You will see many strange and wonderful things
come and go, but you will be still. This is the happiness of the
Buddha.*

AJAHN CHAH, *A Still Forest Pool*

Everything Changes

In the summer of 2006, I took part in a retreat unlike any I had
made before: contemplative kayaking in the wilderness of southeast Alaska. The wilderness setting and kayaking format of the
retreat were both new to me; moreover, it was my first time helping to lead a retreat in the wild. Kurt Hoelting, who had con-
ceived and led these retreats for almost a decade, had invited me
to join him, and we were meeting at his home base in
Petersburg, Alaska, for some planning before the retreat began.
On my flight in, I was aware of a sense of great excitement,
alongside a feeling of not at all knowing what I was getting into.
Our retreat would take place in a part of the Inside Passage
waterway that arcs up the northeast coast from Puget Sound to
southeast Alaska, and Kurt appropriately called the contemplative work of these kayaking retreats "Inside Passages."

I had settled into my window seat on the morning plane from Seattle to Petersburg, and for a time it looked as though the adjoining seats would be unclaimed. Just before the door to the plane closed, however, a mother, infant, and four-year-old boy stumbled aboard. They were the only young family on the plane, and I noted that my heart did not leap up in joy at my good fortune when they dropped into the seats next to mine. A kind passenger offered to hold the infant while the mother got all the family's gear stowed, but as the baby was transferred back to mom, both women uttered, "Uh-oh," at the same instant. The baby had let loose a terrific bowel movement just as the plane was pushing away from the gate.

The four-year-old turned to me and, with weary resignation, observed, "That's a disgusting smell."

I said to him, "Partner, you are right about that."

His mother gave us both a reproachful look.

On flights these days, I notice more passengers using noise-canceling headphones that wrap them in a cocoon of their favorite music during flights. There is to my knowledge, however, no similar smell-canceling apparatus. "Not to worry," I thought to myself, "Surely when the 'fasten seat belt' sign has been turned off, Mom will get up to change the baby."

But no.

This mom was in no rush to remedy the situation. I found myself wondering if this was payback for my simple agreement with the four-year-old. Or maybe, I speculated, Mom no longer had a functioning sniffer after so many diaper changes. Whatever her reason, she was not budging. She and the baby dozed off. The four-year-old also fell asleep, leaning his head against me, and we were flying along like one happy family.

Against this unremitting stench (words to do it justice fail me), I was getting my first views of Alaska out the airplane window: mile after mile of mountains with snow, rivers of ice cutting through the forested landscape, a vastness without any road or sign of human habitation. It was a magnificent view. I was aware of these exceptional sights—and this unfortunate smell.

Byron Katie, a teacher who has been greatly helpful to me, notes in her book *Loving What Is* that when we're in heaven, we say something like, "This is wonderful. I could stay here forever." In hell, the observation is more like, "This is not quite perfect." In all honesty, on the flight to Alaska that morning I was thinking this was not quite perfect.

Hooked by the thought that the mother ought to get up to change the baby, I resisted what was. I asked myself one of the four basic questions from Katie's teachings to check out my assumption: Is this thought true? *Should* the mother get up to change the baby? However much I might wish it, this clearly wasn't happening. I could continue to believe my story that she should, but the effect was only to draw my attention away from the glories out the window. I wanted a different reality. My story about how reality *should* be was not a true story.

I tried out another of Katie's recommended questions: Who or what would I be without this thought? What if I didn't believe that this moment should be different, that the present moment was not quite perfect? Well, for starters, I wouldn't be in contention with this smell. The smell would just be there. I'd be enjoying the scenery and not working myself up with a story that the mother should bloody well get moving and change that baby. Or maybe I'd take action and simply ask the mother if she would mind changing her baby: "Excuse me, I was noticing a smell and wondered if you would mind changing your baby?" Or (turning the thought that she should change her baby around), *I* could even offer to change the baby! "Ma'am, this may seem a bit forward to you, but would you mind if I changed your baby?" After all, I did have considerable experience in the baby-changing line of work. Somehow the last option seemed intrusive into her custody of the little one, but knowing that I had some options made me feel less like a prisoner on the flight.

Pondering these options, I found another solution: by looking out the window and breathing into my sleeve, the whole situation became quite manageable. A handkerchief over my face, outlaw-style, would have been too dramatic, I reasoned, and might possibly draw unnecessary attention from an air marshal, though it could have sent a signal to Mom (though perhaps too subtle a signal for this mom, I thought). Anyway, I was no longer in contention with the smell-reality and rather pleased at my inventiveness. About the time I became satisfied with this solution, the truth of impermanence came to my rescue, the truth that nothing lasts forever. Shunryu Suzuki, founder of the San Francisco Zen Center, was once asked if he could sum up Buddhism in just a few words. Suzuki Roshi thought for a moment and replied, "Everything changes." Indeed.

The mother suddenly lurched out of the seat toward the lavatory in the rear, and the four-year-old turned to me and announced with a satisfied smile, "My brother just peed on my mother."

"Ah," I said. "Babies will do that, won't they?"

"Yep, they sure will," he nodded knowingly.

He and I had become deeply bonded with one another by now. Mom returned with a freshly changed baby but an unhappy countenance. On we flew.

My family flying companions got off the plane (oh, happy day) at Ketchikan, where to my amazement there were bald eagles standing on the runway, as if awaiting orders from air traffic control. Having never seen a bald eagle before, it was a moment to appreciate. As Vietnamese Zen master Thich Nhat Hanh teaches, I began breathing in, "How amazing!" And breathing out, "Smile." Breathing and smiling, an all-purpose way to meet any moment mindfully. It was nice to be able to breathe freely again—bigger smile. After waiting for the weather to clear sufficiently for us to land in Petersburg, we took off again and were at our destination in a matter of minutes. My friend and co-leader of the trip, Kurt, was waiting at the airport, and we were soon in his skiff, heading down the Wrangell Narrows to his cabin, a thirty-minute boat ride from town. By that afternoon, Kurt had me in a sea kayak, paddling with him in and out of quiet estuaries.

The Heart of Mindfulness

This was my first time in Alaska, and it seemed to me as though we were paddling through a Tang dynasty scroll. Cloud-hung mountains came right down to the water. The occasional human being boating across the water was tiny in the vastness of the landscape. We floated past the trunk of a tree where someone had nailed an enormous whale skull.

Enormous, too, was the silence of the place. There were no mechanized sounds, just water sounds, wind sounds, eagle sounds, all coming from and disappearing into the great silence. I thought again of Byron Katie and heaven: "This is wonderful. I could stay here forever." Breathing in, "Happiness is like this." Breathing out, "Smile." Just breathing, floating, smiling, happy. Nothing else was necessary.

But since, as Buddhism teaches, everything changes, so does the mind with happiness. After a while, I found myself wanting just a little bit more happiness. Buddhists call this the "grasping mind," and it is this grasping that leads to suffering and stepping on the wheel of samsara, the endless cycle of birth and death. The grasping mind was wanting just a little bit more. The thought came to me, "I wish Alex [my son] and Kathy [my wife] could see this." How quickly on the heels of happiness comes an improving thought: "This could be even better." Mind with happiness becomes mind with improving—a slight bit of resisting what is.

When we are able to watch our minds, we can notice that different thoughts come and go. Who knows where these thoughts come from or where they go? Usually this coming and going of thoughts happens out of our awareness, but with mindfulness practice, we can take notice and watch. Watching thoughts is like watching boats moving past our view on the water: "Here comes the 'improving' boat; there goes the 'it's-not-quite-right' boat." By *knowing* that the mind has moved to improving, we can *choose* whether to follow this improving thought or to simply watch the urge to improve arise and let it be, without having to take action or fix anything.

In its essence, mindfulness is the intention to be aware, whatever we are doing. Mindfulness is knowing our experience. Like the commercial that asks, "What's in *your* wallet?" mindfulness practice offers us the chance to know, "What's in *your* mind?"

Someone once asked the Buddha what it was he and his disciples did. He replied that they sat, walked, and ate. When asked what was so remarkable about that, he said, "When we sit, we *know* we are sitting. When we walk, we *know* we are walking. When we eat, we *know* we are eating." This intention to be aware of the simplest everyday movements of body and mind is the heart of mindfulness. In fact, the Buddha once said that if we were to maintain this moment-to-present-moment awareness for a week, we would be enlightened. This present-moment awareness, and the peace and joy that come with it, is what Thich Nhat Hanh calls "the miracle of mindfulness."

Paddling that afternoon, when I stopped to pay attention to the improving thought in my mind, I was able to let it be, and in time, it let go of me. Could Alex and Kathy be here with me now? No. More to the point, could *I* be here now? With this question, something shifted inside me. Being here now happened, and letting go of improving happened, and a little movement of energy flowed through my torso with this release. I came back to the feeling of the paddle in my hands, the sound of the paddle in and out of the water, the rhythm of my breathing. I thought of what one of my Buddhist teachers often says: "Be here now. Be some-place else later." Smile.

The Weakest Link

The next day we took the skiff back to town and met the rest of our group, a band of twelve, all but one of us ordained ministers in various Christian traditions: Methodist, Presbyterian, Episcopalian, Disciples of Christ, and Congregationalist. While everyone knew someone on the trip, nobody previously knew everyone. Before coming to Alaska, however, we had exchanged pre-trip reflections by e-mail to get acquainted. One of our group, Anna, wrote this:

> Hey, everybody! I've been holding off on writing my own pre-trip reflections for awhile—probably because I've been trying to live in denial that I'm actually going to go on the trip. Unlike others who have shared their anticipation about this trip, I myself am scared to go. I have no experience in the wilderness at all, and no kayaking skills to speak of. I have a full-time pastorate and a husband and two-year-old daughter. Although it's a lot to handle at times, I feel like I've finally found a good balance. I am "competent" in every area of my life and feel secure in it ... which is why I'm FREAKING OUT about this trip—because I know I will be supremely INcompetent in Alaska.
>
> I know this was the reason I signed up in the first place, because I believe in the power of a true wilderness experience. I believe that when we are at our weakest and our most vulnerable, we can experience God in an entirely new way. I've been in the "wilderness" before at different times of my life, so I know it's true—but that doesn't make it any easier now.

> I told my husband this morning that I don't want to go
> on the trip because I know I'll be the weakest link, and I
> hate that. I hate the idea of the entire group (of strangers,
> no less) looking at me, knowing that I'm the reason we
> move so slowly or need to stop early.

The weakest link. Anna's honesty struck a chord with us all.
Each of us in our different ways carried fears to Alaska; some we
had carried with us long before the trip, some particular to the
trip. None of us wanted to be the weakest link. Anna had named
a fear that in some way was present in us all, and her naming it
helped us relax about it. In our e-mail exchanges, we began to
call ourselves "The Weak Links." The fears of not being enough,
not having enough, not doing enough, not carrying enough of
our weight on this journey were common to us all in differing
degree.

We also had our own idiosyncratic fears. One participant,
whose nephew had nearly drowned her while teaching her
basic kayaking skills before the trip, arrived with a fear for her
safety on the water. We were way off the grid out in the wilderness, and our families had added their fears to the mix with
questions such as, "Will you have a satellite telephone? Will
someone have medical training? What if we need to be in contact with you?" My cousin, himself a collegiate swimmer, had
asked me if I was a strong swimmer. "Absolutely," I had replied.
Inwardly, I was not so sure. But Kurt put many of our fears
about safety to rest at our first meeting. He let us know he
would take no chances. As a veteran fisherman, he had respect
for the weather and for the limitations and experience level of
the group.

The day after we gathered in Petersburg, we took a floatplane the fifty miles to Tebenkof Bay, where we would be spending the next week. The flight through clearing clouds was
spectacular, with silver light shimmering off the water. As we

descended into base camp, we could see groups of sea otters gathered together in the water. The floatplane touched down so smoothly that our landing was imperceptible. After we unloaded our gear, the plane was soon speeding across the water to lift off for other errands, leaving us in the great silence of the place. After months of preparation, our trip was underway.

Each day, our routine went something like this. We would rise at 5:30 a.m., and after our morning ablutions, Kurt would lead the group in the basics of sitting and walking meditation. We would sit in a circle on the rocky beach for a thirty-minute guided meditation, do mindful walking for thirty minutes more, and then sit in meditation for another half hour. Over hot drinks we would talk about what we were noticing in our mindfulness practice. Those new to sitting meditation were going though the agonies of trying to find a comfortable sitting position, and even the veteran meditators were going though the usual physical shakedown that comes with spending extended time in motionless sitting. After breakfast we would set out in our kayaks, find a rhythm of paddling in silence for thirty to forty-five minutes, and then float wordlessly for half an hour. We would paddle until lunchtime, when we would stop and eat on an island. Then we would paddle back to camp or make a new camp farther along our route. When we'd finished kayaking for the day, I would lead the group in the mindful movement of qigong in silence on the beach. Our bodies were always grateful for the slow, restorative movements of qigong.

After dinner we'd gather around the campfire and sit in meditation again. To help us listen to one another, we followed the Native American practice of the talking stick, where the person who holds the stick is the only one who can speak. Silence and speech alternated as we sat around the embers of the fire, until at last we "weak links" would head to our tents, often bedding down to the breathing sounds of humpback whales over the water.

Small Mind, Big Mind

Each day the retreat offered us the chance to engage in mindfulness practice, in moment-to-moment attentiveness, from either
a tightly focused or a wide-angle awareness. For any stretch of
time, we could choose to anchor attention closely on sensations
in the body or on the in-and-out flow of the breath. We might
choose, for instance, to be aware of sensations in our hands
through the various activities of the day or, as best we could, our
breathing in and out all day long. Or we might choose to rest in
wide-angle "choiceless awareness," watching as breath, sensation, sound, thought, or sight arrived in ever-changing flow. In
this wide-angle mode, we could silently note in our minds,
"breathing … sensing … hearing … thinking … feeling … seeing."
Each gentle observation invited us to experience whatever might
be arriving in the present moment.

The awareness of the breath or sensation or mental activity
is not an end in itself, but a means of being present, of waking
up to the present moment. As Thich Nhat Hanh likes to say, our
appointment with life is in the present moment. Whether our
present-moment awareness is microscopic (feeling the breath at
the rim of the nostrils) or panoramic (listening to the soundscape), we get to watch the play of what Buddhists call "small
mind" and "big mind."

Small mind is the narrow, grasping mind, reaching out
whenever it can for pleasure, praise, recognition, or gain. Small
mind reflexively grasps for what it believes will bring happiness
and pushes away what it believes will bring pain. The little crabs
in the tidal pools of Tebenkof Bay, their claws reaching skyward,
seemed the perfect representation of small mind. Watching my
own small mind's pincers open and close on what it wanted at
the moment—whether it was a more comfortable sleeping bag
spot or less snoring from the tent next door, or more of a particular kind of food or a warmer or cooler temperature—I saw all

the big and little ways I was in contention with reality. Small mind, resisting what is, wants just a little bit more or just a little bit less. Small mind is all about "me and mine," what I'm getting and what I'm not getting. Small mind, because of its egocentric sightlines, has been likened to looking at reality through a pinhole, the pinhole of what you want or resist.

Big mind, on the other hand, is open to what is. Because it knows the truth of impermanence, that everything changes, big mind knows that pleasure does not come without pain, that praise does not come without blame, that gain does not come without loss, that recognition does not come without disgrace. These Eight Vicissitudes, as the Buddha called them, inevitably come conjoined as "terrible twins," though we might wish them separate, we don't get one without the other. Big mind is open to the full play of pleasant, unpleasant, and neutral events, but small mind wants only the pleasant and inevitably suffers when reality brings pain, blame, loss, or disgrace instead. Buddhist teachers compare small mind to a little container, a cup, into which a handful of salt has been dropped. Big mind, by contrast, receives the same salt of experience, but the salt can diffuse into great spaciousness, like the wide waters of Tebenkof Bay.

Again and again on the Alaska retreat, I got to see how mindfulness could convert the narrow grasping of small mind to the spacious openness of big mind. The Tibetan teacher Chögyam Trungpa used to say, "There is no cure for hot and cold." Hot and cold just happen—that's the way things are. My small mind, experiencing temperatures in the forties in the morning, had little desire to get out of my warm sleeping bag for early meditation. Noticing my resistance to the cold, I asked myself, where is this resistance in my body? Inevitably, with resistance there is some tightening, some musculoskeletal contraction. When I noticed this tightening in my shoulders and opened with curiosity to the feeling of the contraction in my body, something shifted internally. Spaciousness arose from mindfulness, a mental alternative to silently griping about how cold it was. Small mind, when observed with nonjudgment and curiosity, gives way to big mind. The morning was still cold, but I now held it in a larger space of awareness.

One morning we awoke to clouds, wind, and light rain, and I expected we might meditate inside a communal tent that we used in bad weather, but Kurt took our circle outside to sit on the beach. Dressed warmly in fleece and rain gear, it was surprisingly comfortable to meditate in the rain, even with winds whipping at our clothing. Sitting there, I was reminded of mindfulness teacher Jon Kabat-Zinn's "Mountain Meditation" teaching in *Wherever You Go, There You Are*: a mountain "just sits," receiving any kind of weather, without complaint. The mountains around me were just sitting. As we dropped into the meditation that morning, my body felt as stable and rooted as a mountain, and the sitting felt as though it could have gone on for hours. "Just sitting" comfortably in the rain is impossible in the space of constricted awareness, but in the space of big mind there are possibilities never available to the small mind.

"Let the emptiness breathe you," was the meditation instruction for the day. There is a profound letting go that comes when the body is effortlessly "being breathed" rather than working at watching the breath. As I sat there that morning with eyes open, a soft-eyed gaze focusing on no object in particular, only the empty space between objects, I felt as though the spaciousness of big mind were breathing me. The spaciousness and emptiness were not just "out there"—they were inside me as well.

This was a blissful sitting, one with quiet, energetic wakefulness and equanimity. Who knew that sitting in the rain could be like this? Kurt had said before the trip that this territory was "big medicine," and, indeed, I was finding it so. Big mind, big medicine.

Renunciation Practice

Not everyone in our group was enjoying "just sitting" in the rain. A few days into the retreat, while one person reported that he was "drinking in the silence," Anna acknowledged that she was "really struggling." In particular, the paddling was physically demanding, and the silence was intensifying the struggle in her mind. Our rule of silence left her without the usual outlets of conversation or complaint. With no conversation allowed, silence contained and echoed the chatter in her mind.

Mindfulness retreats, my Buddhist teachers often remind me, are practice in renunciation. On retreat we renounce certain comforts, pleasures, and most of all, our customary distractions. There are no screens on retreat: no computer, television, or video games. Reading and even writing are discouraged; there is nothing to distract us from the central practice of paying attention to whatever is arising in the present moment. We are asked to notice: What is happening now? And now? And now? Be here now, be someplace else later. Is that so hard? You have to try it yourself to discover just how challenging this simple practice can be, how little time we humans spend in the present moment, how seductive past and future are to minds deluged with distraction.

The renunciations of the retreat in Alaska allowed Anna to come to a discovery about the nature of the mind and how her mind worked. Before this retreat, whenever she found herself struggling, she would try her best to struggle out of the struggle, or, failing that, to turn her attention away from it. Out in the wilderness, she found that neither continuing to struggle nor attempting mental distraction was helping her. These strategies only increased her frustration with the experience. Eventually, however, she hit upon a third way: simply letting herself *have* the experience. She tried watching her struggling and, by holding her experience in awareness, came to see, "Struggling is like this." Rather than fighting against her physical discomfort, she allowed herself to *have* the experience of struggling to find a comfortable rhythm in paddling. This simple shift gave rise to the insight that she did not have to struggle against something unpleasant. She could choose to notice, "Unpleasantness is like this." She could drop her story about "I hate this and when is it going to end?" and, instead, bring curiosity to how her mind and body reacted to her story of unpleasantness.

Anna already knew about herself that whenever something was "not right," she had a habit of trying to fix it, whether for herself or someone else. She could see this fixing habit in her life as a mother and as a minister. But when her fix didn't work, she would find herself frustrated, discouraged and, in time, resentful. These variations on resistance were arising in her on this wilderness retreat. What mindfulness showed her was that there was another way. She could allow her experience of struggle to happen and neither fix nor fight it, but hold it with the same tenderness she gave to her two-year-old daughter back home. By letting herself have her experience without judging it, holding it in awareness, in time she found a rhythm and power in paddling that were her own. In making this discovery, she wondered what it might be like back home to approach her struggles there in this different, mindful way, to say to herself, "Okay, struggling is happening. What is this like in my mind and body?"

Renunciation practices, such as the Christian practice of giving up of certain pleasures or habits during Lent, are available in our day, but they are neither prominent nor especially powerful means of insight for many Christians. From earlier times, especially among the Christian Desert Mothers and Fathers of fourth- and fifth-century Syria, Palestine, and Egypt, a remarkable body of wise sayings and teachings on renunciation has been collected. These teachings comprise ancient Christian wisdom on how to work with the energies released in the mind and the body through renunciation practices. In both their Christian and Buddhist forms, renunciation practices can become powerful avenues for insight because they put our mental habits of grasping and attachment on display, where we can simply observe them.

In one of the Christian desert stories, it is said that a monk went to see Abba Moses and begged him for a word of teaching. The old man told him to go and sit in his cell, that his cell would teach him everything.

Doing as he was instructed, the monk sat in his hermitage cell, where he began to encounter his "demons and wild beasts," as the Christian contemplatives called them. He met his own greed, boredom, anger, inferiority, sadness, despair, superiority, and the dreaded "noonday demon," which the monks called *accedia*—an inertia so profound that it leaves one without the strength left to bury the dead. Buddhist teaching calls these mental states variations of the Five Hindrances: grasping, aversion, restlessness, fatigue, and doubt—all hindrances to clear seeing.

In both Buddhist and Christian traditions, the renunciations of silence, sitting still, and watchfulness together create what psychotherapists call a "container" in which difficult mind states or hindrances can arise and be transformed through the alchemy of practice. When we go on a retreat today, whatever we hope to leave behind by going into the wilderness invariably accompanies us, shadowlike in its refusal to leave, just as it did for the monks in the desert fifteen hundred years ago. There are great energies locked in this shadow, energies that can be freed by the nonjudgment and kind observation of mindfulness practice. Our mental habits of judgment, irritation, complaint, insecurity, restlessness, doubt—variants of wanting what isn't and resisting what is—can raise quite a ruckus in our minds!

At the beginning of any retreat, the outer silence of a desert or wilderness often exposes not inner calm but a distressing degree of noise and struggle, as it did for Anna. It usually requires diligent practice to mirror the outer silence of the desert or the wilderness in our interior silence and equanimity. It is said about one Desert Father, Abba Agathon, that he carried a pebble in his mouth for three years until he learned to be silent. Although our little kayaking band of twelve did not attempt three years of silence, even a week in our Alaskan "cells" of tent and kayak taught us a few things about the demons and wild beasts of our own minds.

A Refuge from Words

The great teacher in Alaska is the wilderness itself: the vastness of the space, the variability of the weather, and the great variety of life in many rare and precious forms. Tebenkof Bay Wilderness is a temperate rain forest, with enormous Sitka spruce, delicate wildflowers, and luxurious mosses. It is the home of black bear, wolf, and blacktail deer. The raven and eagle overhead once gave their names to the clans of the Tlingit people, who thrived here until their contact with smallpox in the 1830s. The Tlingits said that a man would have to be an imbecile to starve here. They fed themselves from the sea and built a culture aligned with the life cycle of what they called "the salmon people."

One morning Kurt took us on a paddle to some of the places where the Tlingits had lived and fished. Paddling in the rain, we made our way past island after silent island where Tlingits had once made their homes. The rain made perfect concentric circles as it hit the water's surface, each circle holding a little splash rising from its center. From time to time, seals would surface their heads above the water, looking remarkably like black Labrador retrievers, watching us until we made eye contact, then slipping silently below the surface. In the slow-moving beauty of cloud-on-mountain, the peekaboo presence of the seals, the surround sound of rain intensifying and slackening, I thought to myself, "This is wonderful. I could stay here forever." I threw back the hood of my rain jacket and paddled bareheaded in the rain. A bald eagle hit the water and rose into the air with a silver salmon in its talons.

Just when I thought it couldn't get any more wonderful, we heard a big breath sound behind us. Without even needing to turn around, we knew it was a whale. A giant humpback surfaced not thirty yards from our boats, exhaling a plume of spray. For a good while it kept pilgrimage with us, an awesome companion, so close its barnacles were in plain view. And then it departed. The rising of its great fluke above the water's surface, then its disappearing, were as majestic and mysterious as any thing I'd ever seen. *Emma Ho,* the Tibetans say. How amazing! My hands came together in the greeting of *namasté*—"the divine light in me greets the divine light in you"—acknowledging this great being that had graced us with its presence.

Hearing the humpback's exhale, watching the spray of its plume recede into the distance, I was reminded of the Unnamable One's question to Job in that great hymn to creation that came out of the whirlwind: "Can you draw out Leviathan with a hook?" The voice asked if Job had entered into the springs of the sea or walked in the recesses of the deep. Had he entered into the storehouses of the snow? Was it at *Job's* command that the eagle mounts up and makes his nest on high? (Job 41:1, 38:16, 38:22, and 39:27) Like Job, I felt a deep reverence for the loveliness and grace of this wilderness experience—and my own smallness in comparison.

We had seen deer and eagle, sea otter and seal, salmon and black bear. We had gone to sleep with the sounds of the humpback whales. Paddling through this wilderness preserve, we had witnessed the great energies of creation. Then one afternoon Kurt took us and our kayaks to the edge of the wilder waters of Chatham Strait. We quickly knew in our bodies just how insignificant our little boats and our strength were in the neighborhood of such powerful energies. Like Job, we were in the face of something far beyond words.

After I had returned home, a friend told me about another group of Christians who had been traveling in Alaska. They, too, had been awed by what they had seen as they looked down on one of the great glaciers. In response, one of their group, a minister, had suggested they celebrate the Eucharist, the central act of Christian worship. Others of the group had a different intuition, but reluctant to disagree, they went along. Later, these others wished they had spoken about their reservations because they had experienced the service as something "not quite right." The scene asked for silence, not words—not even holy words.

In *Nine-Headed Dragon River*, the writer and Zen practitioner Peter Matthiessen tells a story told by his teacher, Soen Roshi, that shows how words can get in the way of the natural expression of the scene itself:

> One day a young monk had a *kensho* [an initial awakening experience] and his teacher, seeking to deepen this experience, led him on a long walk up Mount Fuji. Although the monk had seen the great snow mountain many times before, he truly perceived it now for the first time ... all the way up, he kept exclaiming over the harmony and colors of the wildflowers, the flight of birds, the morning light in the fresh evergreens, the sacred white mountain rising in mighty silence to the sky. "Look, Roshi, this pinecone! See how it is made? This stone, it's so ... *stone*! Isn't it wonderful? Do you hear the nightingale? It's a miracle! Oh! Fuji-san!"
>
> Muttering a little, the old master hobbled onward, until finally his student noticed his long silence and cried out, "Isn't it so? Aren't these mountains, rivers, and great earth miraculous? Isn't it beautiful?"

The old man turned on him. "Yes-s-s," he said force-fully. "But what a pity to say so!"

Indeed. What a pity to say so. Buddhists have a saying, "The fin-ger pointing at the moon is not itself the moon." Words are often like the finger pointing at the moon; they are not the thing itself. While Christian contemplatives are not strangers to silence, most of us Christians are far more accustomed to words than silence: words from sacred scriptures, words in sermon and wor-ship, words about the Word. Part of the pull of Buddhist prac-tice for me is the refuge it offers from words, creeds, and doctrines. In the experience of silence, and whatever arises in it, I find a blessed relief from religious words, from the stories we tell ourselves about our words, and from our life-and-death attachment to our stories.

Father Thomas Keating, Trappist monk and teacher of cen-tering prayer, reminds us that God's first word is silence. That it is out of silence that the Word is born. In Alaska, the silence allowed each of us to experience the thing itself—the whale, the rain, being comfortable, being uncomfortable, moments of fear, moments of freedom—without an immediate overlay of words or interpretation from anyone else. Twice a day, over hot tea in the morning and around the campfire at night, we had the chance to give words to our experience, but only after we had sat with it for a time in silence. In those times of speaking, authen-tic words, words of honest emotion rang true. Preachy words, as they always do, rang hollow. As our silence deepened, so did the authenticity of our words, fewer and truer.

Dropping into Freedom

While there were many sacred moments for us in Alaska, one stands above all in my mind, with a certain melancholy. Two hundred years ago, before contact with white people, there were thousands of Tlingit people throughout the islands of southeast Alaska. Today there are none in this area, though Tlingits live elsewhere in Alaska. Kurt took us to archaeological sites where Tlingit villages had once thrived; now there are only impressions in the earth where their homes once stood.

On the last day of our trip, we paddled to a small island near our base camp. Several deer watched us as we pulled our kayaks ashore. We made our way from the beach into the rain forest and came upon a lone totem pole standing among the trees, facing out to sea. As we approached the carving, I had the sense that I was approaching what Celtic Christians called a "thin place," a spot where the Presence is so strong it feels like a portal between worlds. I thought of Moses standing before the burning bush: "Take off your shoes, for the ground on which you are standing is holy" (Exodus 3:5).

We stood for a good while in silence around the totem pole. It bore the marks of weather and decay, and I wondered how much longer it would be standing. Elsewhere on the island was a shaman's recent grave, but Kurt said it was best not to go there because the Tlingits didn't want us coming to that spot. This place belonged to them, not to us. In all this bountiful vastness, this small island is the one place in the wilderness the Tlingit people have claimed as their own. Here in this deep silence they come to bury their shamans, those travelers between the natural and the spirit worlds. That the Tlingits are all but gone from this part of Alaska was a melancholy reminder of how ignorantly and cruelly we can treat each other by separating ourselves into "us" and "them." This decaying totem pole seemed to say, "Enjoy your fleeting connections to all beings and to this stunningly beautiful earth. Be mindful of them, and treat them well."

Spirit Rock Meditation Center's founding teacher, Jack Kornfield, tells an us-and-them story from the Zen tradition. It's a story about dropping whatever burden you are carrying: your thoughts, your story, your identity, your plans, your judgments, your regrets, your sense of separation into "us" and "them." It's a story about coming out of small mind into big mind:

There was an old monk in China who practiced very hard meditation for many years. He had a good mind, became very quiet, had good meditation, but yet never came ... to that source of complete stillness or peace.... So he went to the Zen master and said, "May I please have permission to go off and practice in the mountains? I've worked for years as a monk and there's nothing else I want but to understand this: the true nature of myself, of this world." The master, knowing that he was ripe, gave him permission to leave.

The monk left the monastery and took his bowl and his few possessions and walked through the various towns to the mountains. He left the last village behind and was going up a little trail into the mountains. Coming down the trail, an old man appeared before him, carrying a great big bundle on his back. This old man was actually the Bodhisattva Manjusri, who is said to appear to people at the moment they are ripe for awakening and is depicted carrying the sword of discriminating wisdom that cuts through all attachment, all illusion and separateness. The monk looked at the old man, and the old man said, "Say friend, young monk, where are you going?" The monk told his story. "I've practiced for all these years and all I want now is to touch the center point, to know that which is true." The old man looked at him and his look was kind and wise. So the monk said, "Tell me, old man, do you know anything of this enlightenment?" At which point the old man simply let go of the bundle; it dropped to the ground and the monk was enlightened.

That's all. Just put it down. Drop everything: I, my, what I want to be, what I'm going to get, what will happen. Just be here. At this point the newly enlightened monk looked at the old man again, and said, "So now what?" The old man reached down and picked up the bundle again and walked off to town.

Here's the complete teaching in this story. It's to put everything down—all I, all me.... Once you put it down, then with understanding and compassion you can pick it up again.

This was the great gift of our contemplative retreat in Alaska: the freedom to put down the stories of "I and me." In experiences such as watching the great fluke of the humpback whale slide beneath the water's surface, we dropped into a freedom beyond our customary roles and attachments. We came into simple belonging, simply being in this majestic space. It was hard to hold on to the stories of the narrow mind for long in this big medicine place; something was always calling us into a larger view. Contemplative practice is like this: paying attention, noticing you are hooked, opening to how this feels in your body, holding this being hooked with kindness, and watching how your heart opens.

On our last night in Tebenkof Bay, we used the talking stick to speak about what fears had hooked us, what freedoms we had tasted. It was a rich conversation. We'd been hooked by fears of drowning, of being the weakest link, of not being or having or doing enough, of not belonging. We noted how often the landscape had called us out of our fears, our little stories, into big mind. Practicing again and again coming back into the present moment, we had learned that we could trust whatever we found there. We had learned that each moment was manageable, one breath at a time. We had learned that whenever we dropped our stories about how things had been or ought to be, all sorts of possibilities and pleasures came into view.

There was the lone white bird lit by the morning light, flying over the still water. There was the simple pleasure of hot oatmeal in the chill of daybreak. There was the quiet company of the sea otters watching as we paddled past. There were the eagles, lifting our hearts as they soared over our afternoon qigong. There were the mountains, always "just sitting" there. There was our constant companion, the weather, always changing, rain to sun to rain again, bringing new possibilities and challenges. There was the sweet appreciation we had come to feel for each other, for the effort and honesty each of us brought to the retreat. And there was the this-is-the-best-thing-I've-ever-felt gratification of a hot shower at the end of our time in the wilderness. Breathing in, "Pleasure." Breathing out, "Smile."

Back at home on my desk are an eagle feather and two stones from the beaches of Tebenkof Bay. These objects link me to my companions and to moments of mindfulness in Alaska. They remind me of the big mind and the big medicine of freedom, and of my gratitude for this "Inside Passage." They remind me of what the Buddha taught his followers to recite when they were afraid in the wild, to help them drop their story lines of fear:

> *May all beings be safe.*
> *May all beings be at peace.*
> *May all beings be happy.*
> *May all beings be free.*

Blessed Relief: The Three-Minute Breathing Space

You don't need to travel to Alaska to experience the spaciousness of the present moment. You can know this spaciousness right where you are. The Three-Minute Breathing Space can open you from the narrow confines of small mind into the expansiveness of big mind.

Medical researchers have discovered that just three minutes of soft-belly breathing will shut down the stress response and elicit its physiological opposite, the relaxation response. When you concentrate like this, you give yourself a break. You rest the part of you that is busy noticing what is wrong with yourself, with others, or with the situation. You let go of trying to fix yourself, fix someone else, or fix the situation. You rest. Doing this three-minute ritual of recovery every one-and-a-half to two hours can bring calmness and deep refreshment to you. Try it, and see for yourself.

- Bring your body into an upright and dignified sitting position, with both feet on the floor.

- First, listen to sounds. How many different sounds can you hear? As best you can, allow the sounds to be just the way they are.

- After a minute, be aware of sensations in your hands. Feel your hands from the *inside.* Again, allow these sensations to be just the way they are.

- Then shift your attention to your breathing. Notice where you feel your breath most prominently in your body: whether at your nostrils, your rib cage, or your abdomen.

Station your attention at that place. Feel the physical sensations of your breath as it moves in and out of that spot.

- Finally, see if you can be aware of all three at once, like three notes in a musical chord: sounds, sensations in your hands, and the in-out of your breathing.

- Do this for three minutes.

- As you breathe in, imagine inflating a balloon in your belly. As you breathe out, let the breath release from your body on its own, without forcing or pushing it out. Just let go.

2

THE CRY FOR HELP

Almost everyone I've met who has turned to the Buddha did so because they suffered the end of a love affair. They have lost someone they loved. Perhaps they have lost a country as well, or parents or siblings or some function of their bodies. But very often people turn to the Buddha because they have been carried so deeply into their suffering by the loss of a loved one that without major help they fear they will never recover.

ALICE WALKER, "Suffering Too
Insignificant for the Majority to See"

The Why and the What of Suffering

When I was a young theology student, I was struck by how many of my male classmates had suffered some loss in connection with their fathers. For many of us, our fathers were either dead or distant or absent. It would be years before some of us would begin to understand how our losses affected the choices we would make in love and work, but during our schooling we found in each other a fellowship of persons magnetically pulled toward suffering. Along with our theological studies, we worked in hospitals and prisons, with the homeless and the hurting. In my first year of study, a delightful thirteen-year-old girl named Lynn, a real day-brightener and favorite of mine in the parish where I worked, fell ill over a three-month period and died, a brain tumor ending her young life.

I hated that Lynn died and hated how cancer hurt her and her family. Having little sense of how to mourn this loss, and less of how to help her family deal with their loss, I set myself to try to explain the *why* of suffering—if not to them, at least to myself—and to reconcile the evident fact of suffering with Christian testimony to divine loving presence. I took courses in the Wisdom literature and theodicy of the Hebrew Bible. I studied Dostoevsky's *The Brothers Karamozov* and Camus' *The Plague* and read endlessly about the Holocaust. But just beneath this attempt to explain suffering was a visceral refusal of a world in which such things as Lynn's death could happen.

It was suffering that drew me to theological education over thirty years ago, and suffering has been the subject that links the energies of my professional life as a therapist and my spiritual practice. If there is one theme that runs like a red thread through most of the books on my bookshelf, it's the fact of suffering.

Suffering reached out and grabbed me by the throat when I was nineteen, the night two childhood friends died, their car slamming into a tree in my front yard. Since then I've been engaged in what at various times has been a long argument with suffering, sometimes finding myself in a life-and-death struggle with it, sometimes learning how to relieve it, and sometimes simply learning how to sit with it. Huston Smith, the great teacher of comparative religion, once observed that all religions begin with the cry for help. In the face of suffering, what actually helps? And what doesn't?

I'd like to approach these questions with an invitation. After you've read this paragraph, close your eyes for a moment, sit quietly and notice how your body receives your in-breath, and how it releases your out-breath. Then notice what comes to mind with the word *suffering*. What images, what memories, what stories present themselves? As you stoke the material around this word *suffering*, what do you notice happens in your body?

I call this approach to the matter of suffering the "experience near" approach. It is tempting, as I have done in the past, to put a lot of energy into trying to *explain* suffering: explaining *why* suffering happens, explaining why *this* suffering is happening. My own experience has taught me that the turn down the *why* road is a wrong turn. The question *why* is an unsuccessful detour around the implacable *what* of suffering.

An Exit from Hell

Shortly after Hurricane Katrina tore apart the Gulf Coast and flooded New Orleans, I was asked to come to Baton Rouge to work with chaplains and social workers providing care to the emergency responders working in a group of hospitals run by Franciscan sisters. Flying into Baton Rouge a week after the hurricane, I met an Hasidic rabbi from the New York City Office of the Chief Medical Examiner. He had come to help identify unclaimed bodies in the mortuary. This man had seen a lot of suffering in his life, and he knew something about helping people pick up the pieces in the aftermath of devastation.

The population of Baton Rouge had doubled overnight, and needless to say, there were no hotel rooms available anywhere nearby. Some of the hospital staff told me they had as many as twenty or thirty people staying in their homes. I slept on a couch in an empty doctor's office. For days, persons fleeing New Orleans had slept under the ramps of Louisiana State University's Pete Maravich Assembly Center, which served as the largest field hospital for acute care injuries ever created in U.S. history. In eight days the emergency rooms of the Franciscan hospitals alone had seen over three thousand people. And there were three thousand homeless pets in the LSU Agricultural Center.

The blue hospital signs on the interstate, the first ones north of New Orleans, pointed the way to these Franciscan hospitals.

People fleeing New Orleans found an exit from hell, and though their suffering didn't end when they found a hospital, they did find kindness. What responders told me they universally received from those who came for assistance was gratitude beyond words. "Y'all treating us like we're human," was the refrain these helpers heard over and over. One social worker told me she had never seen so much physical trauma, that after a few days she went numb to the spectrum of suffering she witnessed, from the horrific to the frustrating. A nurse who had worked for over forty-eight hours without sleep said her own grief broke through while she was bathing an old man. He had been taken off a bus of nursing home patients, one of whom had died during the trip out of New Orleans. While she was sponge bathing the old man, he softly patted her hand, offering her both comfort and gratitude for her care. An act of kindness from this vulnerable old man just broke her wide open.

Amid all the suffering, powerfully moving reunions—people finding one another again when they feared they never would—were taking place. And there were even, as is so often the case with children, moments of hilarity. As nurses were undressing one little boy out of his filthy clothes and putting him into a hospital gown before he was treated, he yelled out to his younger brother, "Quick! Run for your life! They take your clothes and underwear and don't give them back!"

I was reminded of the Christian ethicist Stanley Hauerwas, who observed that when people are hurting, what they need is not an explanation, but a community capable of helping them to absorb their suffering, helping them to simply cope. And I thought of Herbert Anderson, a wise pastoral theologian, who said that the question in the face of suffering is not, what can we say? but what can we bear to hear?

As staff members were given a safe place to talk about what they had experienced, one woman said after telling her story, "It's all here in my stomach, and I can't face it. I'm numb." Another said, "I didn't realize it's all here in my shoulders—I feel like I've been carrying the weight of the world." As people shared their images of suffering and brought awareness to their breathing, many of them said, "It's like I've forgotten to breathe." When we talked about what hadn't helped and what had, one of the nuns said, "Well, what sure *didn't* help was the visit of the official delegation from the Vatican. They were just in the way. And you know, what *did* help me was a glass of port each night." Nobody in Baton Rouge had a whole lot of energy to try to explain *why* anybody's suffering had come about. They were all about *relieving* suffering as best they could, not explaining it.

My friend Rabbi Rami Shapiro writes in *The Divine Feminine in Biblical Wisdom Literature: Selections Annotated and Explained* (SkyLight Paths): "The way of Wisdom is not the way of why, but the way of what. The Hebrew word [for Wisdom] *chochma* can be read as *choch mah,* 'what is.' Wisdom will not tell you why things are the way they are, but will show you what they are and how you can live in harmony with them." Rami is right. Wisdom teaches us how to live with what is, and when necessary, how to grieve what is. In the process of grieving, we may even come to accept what is—not to like it, but to accept that it has happened, to stop refusing suffering and find how we can live in harmony with it.

In his warm and wise book *Open Secrets,* Rami tells the story of the great Rabbi Akiva, who was once lost in a shipwreck at sea. He alone survived, and when asked how he did it, he replied, "Whenever a wave arose, I bent into it." Rabbi Akiva bent into the wave and it washed over him. As Rami observes, "This is how we are to live in the world, bending into what happens and allowing it to wash over us rather than sweep us away."

But the question is, how do we learn to bend into the wave? How do we learn to give up the habit of refusing what is?

Bearing Suffering

In my youth I had imagined that if somehow I could understand the *why* of suffering, it would hurt less. In time I would learn this was not the case. More than any of my attempts to understand the why of suffering, it was an image of the *what* of suffering that brought an end to my fruitless young efforts to explain suffering. Two years after Lynn's death, I was studying Christian artistic renderings of the life of Jesus, and I saw an image I had never before seen, one so powerful that I came to a different understanding of what helps with suffering. The image was the German artist Matthias Grünewald's sixteenth-century painting *The Crucifixion*. This image was originally part of an altarpiece painted for the Monastery of St. Anthony in Isenheim, Alsace (now in France). The monks of the monastery cared for patients afflicted with what they called St. Anthony's fire, which we now know was an ergot poisoning that afflicted its sufferers with convulsive and gangrenous symptoms. At the center of the Isenheim altarpiece is an enormous, agonized Christ, the weight of his body bowing the crosspiece. The body on the cross is contorted in pain, the flesh stuck with thorns and oozing blood and pus.

When patients at the monastery hospital were brought before the painting, they would have recognized themselves, for the figure before them displayed the very symptoms of their own disease. The patients would have known the one who hung on the cross as one of their own, "a man of suffering and acquainted with infirmity" (Isaiah 53:3). In Grünewald's *Crucifixion* there is no attempt to explain suffering. There is only solidarity with the sufferer. The artist knew that in the face of physical and emotional and spiritual suffering, solidarity helps.

If the dominant image of Christian life is the crucified Christ, the recurring image of Buddhist practice is the Buddha seated in meditation, touching the earth: two very different images, one an image of agony, the other an image of equanimity. But the differences notwithstanding, both are responses to the *what* of suffering. The Buddha's very first teaching to his followers after his enlightenment was the Four Noble Truths about suffering:

> The First Noble Truth: there is suffering *(dukkha)*.
>
> The Second Noble Truth: suffering comes from grasping *(tanha)*.
>
> The Third Noble Truth: there is an end to suffering (nirvana).
>
> The Fourth Noble Truth: there is a way to end suffering (the Eightfold Path).

Our English word *suffering* is a translation of the Pali word *dukkha*, which connotes a wheel that rolls wrongly, off-center from its axle. Think of a grocery cart with wheels that won't roll straight and you get the idea. When our life is off-center and we are in contention with reality, with the way things are, our life rolls wrongly and we suffer. When we believe that something *should* be a certain way, we suffer. When we want something other than *what is,* we suffer.

Sylvia Boorstein, a member of the Spirit Rock Meditation Center's teacher's council and author of *Happiness Is an Inside Job,* sums up the experience of suffering in four words: "Suffering is wanting other." This is the raw material of all suffering: *wanting* reality to be *other* than it is. Thinking that this reality should be different, this moment should be different, this person should be different, I should be different, the world should be different—this is suffering. When we are in contention with reality, when we are "wanting other," we "take birth," as Buddhists say, into suffering.

How many times a day do you find yourself wanting "other," arguing with reality, wanting what isn't and resisting what is, whether the matter is truly terrible or merely trivial?

Here's an exercise I use to help people get a sense of just how powerful this habit of wanting other really is: Carry a three-by-five-inch card with you for each day of one week and make a mark on it each time you find yourself wanting other. When you want the traffic other, the weather other, the political landscape other, your loved ones other, your body other, social injustice other, just make a mark. Add up the marks at the end of the week and see how the numbers are trending. One person given this assignment in one of my stress reduction classes said, "A three-by-five card—forget it. I'll need a legal pad!"

The Greek philosopher Epictetus said, "We are disturbed not by what happens to us, but by our *thoughts* about what happens." The raw material of pain, what happens to the body or in the mind, may range in intensity, but at the core of our suffering is the *thought* that reality should be different.

When I first heard Sylvia Boorstein say that pain is inevitable, but suffering is optional, I thought to myself, could this be true? How is suffering in any way optional? In my experience as a priest and psychotherapist, I had learned that attempts to *explain* suffering, to figure out the *why* of suffering are rarely, if ever, helpful. The book of Job is an extended conversation on the uselessness, even the blasphemy, of "explaining" suffering. I knew from my own experience and from walking with others that when we are in the fire of suffering, what we need is not an explanation but the companionship of people who will walk with us as we work through to the other side of our suffering. Compassionate company can help us bear the weight of suffering, as the Latin *sufferre*, "to bear under," suggests. But is suffering optional?

Sadly, some suffering can only be borne, not relieved, though we must certainly try to bring relief. The image of Jesus bearing his own cross, and crucified, is an archetypal image of a person bearing his own suffering. The patients at St. Anthony's beheld the image of one who did not refuse his suffering, but bore it. Suffering nobly borne may lead to wisdom, or redemption. But some suffering leads to neither. The Buddhist teacher Ajahn Chah wisely said that there are two kinds of suffering: suffering that leads to more suffering, and suffering that leads to freedom. Whether we find freedom or wisdom or redemption, what helps in Buddhist and Greek and Christian teaching is not so much an *explanation* of suffering as a *way to follow* when suffering has come upon us.

When we are hurting, ritual may comfort us. Belief may console us. Philosophy may help us, though C. S. Lewis famously said, "There never was the philosopher who could patiently endure the toothache." What Buddhist teachers bring to the journey with suffering are a host of practices that offer blessed relief from the agonies of the suffering mind and heart and soul. The novelist Alice Walker, not herself a Buddhist, says she has found support "beyond measure" for her own suffering from the teachings of the Buddha. This has been my experience as well.

When Sylvia Boorstein says that pain is inevitable, but suffering is optional, I understand her to say that human beings and human bodies are heir to a host of pains, physical, emotional, and spiritual. These pains come with the fact of incarnation, with the package of this "precious human birth," as Buddhists call it. We have pain because we have bodies and because we have relationships, both of which sometimes bring us pleasure and sometimes bring us pain. But suffering, in the Buddha's teaching, is what we *add* to the pain. Suffering is our thoughts and stories about whatever is happening, our *resistance* to what is. In the Buddhist account, it is this resistance that is at the heart of suffering.

If it's true that pain is inevitable and suffering is optional, then a possibility for genuine freedom arises in how we choose to respond to pain. Pain does not necessarily need to lead to suffering, though the two are often linked as though they were one: pain-and-suffering. If we can learn to distinguish the two, a different possibility opens up, a possibility that is as liberating as it is challenging. This possibility is the freedom of becoming responsible for our mind states, no matter what the situation.

"Responsible for our mind states"—what does this mean? It means that no one else is responsible for your thoughts and stories, for your reactions to painful stimuli. When someone has done something that upsets you, they did not "do it to you." When disaster strikes you or someone else, you do not have to resort to the explanation that God did this to you or someone else. Pain may come your way, but you do not have to add to this pain the suffering of thoughts and stories about why it happened and what should or should not be happening. If those thoughts and stories of suffering do arise, you can learn to work mindfully, skillfully (as Buddhist teachers say) with your thoughts or feelings. While you cannot control what thoughts or feelings arise in the mind stream, you are in charge of what you do with what has arisen.

The Work

Jack Kornfield observes that "Questioning our thoughts is at the heart of Buddhist practice." One teacher who has helped me work with thoughts that lead to suffering is Byron Katie. Katie, as she prefers to be called, had an awakening experience from her own suffering when she saw, very clearly, that when her thoughts were in contention with reality, she suffered. When she questioned those thoughts and asked what was true, her suffering ended. That was it. For her, it was a personal, powerful discovery of the Four Noble Truths: there is suffering, the cause of suffering is grasping, suffering can end, and there is a path to the end of suffering.

There was suffering for Katie when she believed her thoughts, her stories about what was wrong with her life. If she believed her thinking that something *should* be the case, there was suffering. If she was grasping for a different reality, she was suffering. To use a different word, perhaps not as loaded as the word *suffering*, when she was in contention with reality, life was *unsatisfactory* for her.

When Katie began to question her thoughts and stories about reality, she was able to drop the stories and judgments; instead of believing them, she could step aside from her thoughts. As they dropped away, so did her suffering. Now, when asked whether she is enlightened, she responds, "I'm just someone who knows the difference between what hurts and what doesn't." What helped her know this difference was questioning her thoughts, a process she has come to call "The Work." This is a simple yet powerful method of inquiry that I've found very helpful in dealing with suffering.

The first phase of The Work invites us to go ahead and "judge your neighbor," as Katie puts it, to judge reality. This is an invitation to be as petty, judgmental, and unkind as we often silently (or not so silently) are about people or events in our life, and to put these judgments on paper. In essence, these judgments are about how others *should* and *should not be*, how reality *should* and *should not be*.

Once we write our judging thoughts down, we can take our time investigating them. The second phase of The Work is a matter of asking ourselves four questions and writing our responses to each:

1. Is it true?
2. Can I absolutely know that this is true?
3. How do I react when I think this thought?
4. Who or what would I be without the thought?

The last phase of The Work is what Katie calls a turnaround. This is an opportunity to test out the exact opposite of our original thoughts and see what we have in common with the person we have been judging. In a helpful insight in her book *Loving What Is*, Katie explains:

What The Work gives us is a way to change the projector—mind—rather than the projected. It's like when
there is a piece of lint on the projector's lens. We think
there is a flaw on the screen, and we try to change this
person and that person, whomever the flaw appears to be
on next. But it's futile to try to change the projected
images. Once we realize where the lint is, we can clear
the lens itself. This is the end of suffering, and the beginning of a little joy in paradise.

Clearing the Lens

Before I came to mindfulness practices, I generally saw myself
as having the intention to be kind to others, but my thoughts
and actions, perhaps like yours, sometimes fell short of my
intentions. Now some years into mindfulness practice, I am
more aware of the many ways I contract and judge, criticize and
improve in my mind with stories about what is wrong with others and with myself. As Zen teacher John Tarrant says, "My
ordinary thoughts can have a certain amount of refusal in
them."

Watching how and when these judging energies arise, taking responsibility for my own states of mind, and then applying
antidotes to these habits of mind is frankly a work in progress.
But I also see that kindness and compassion, joy and equanimity are capacities of mind that can be further developed with
mindfulness practice. It first takes a willingness to clear the lens
of the projector.

Someone once told the Dalai Lama that he felt very discouraged in his practice, that after years of effort he was making
little progress. The Dalai Lama replied, "I know exactly what you
mean—sometimes I feel just the same way! However, when I
look back over ten, fifteen, twenty years, I feel that some

progress has been made." For myself, I can see that I do some things differently now because of mindfulness practice. At least now I *know* that I am judging and can make a choice whether or not to continue down the path of judgment. At least I know that choosing to continue judging and projecting is, as Buddhist teacher Pema Chödrön says, like choosing to eat rat poison and hoping the rat will die.

For Christians, forgiveness is the heart of Jesus's teaching and the core of Christian practice. Yet the opposite of forgiveness—judgment—is a particular form of human suffering that I suspect many of us practice much more than we do forgiveness. Do any of the following judgments sound familiar to you?

> She should be more considerate ...
>
> I really need to lose some weight ...
>
> It's too hot/cold/dry/wet/gloomy/bright ...
>
> He needs to be more disciplined ...
>
> I'm too quiet/loud/stupid/busy/boring ...
>
> You're too quiet/loud/stupid/busy/boring ...
>
> He's an idiot ...
>
> I'm an idiot ...

Judgments can feel quite personal. After all, it's my judgment about you or your judgment about me that causes us to contract, defend, withdraw, or attack. But the energy of judgment is actually quite impersonal. It can be very helpful to view the activities of the mind, especially thoughts and feelings, not personally, as *me* or *mine*, but impersonally, as *the* thought or *the* feeling. For example, seeing these energies as *the* judgment, *the* anger, *the* depression, and *the* jealousy instead of *my* judgment provides us a little distance from them. From this distance, we can actually begin to work with the judgments, instead of being impossibly entangled and identified with them, as we are when we view them as personal faults.

When you notice that your judging mind is activated, you can note its presence with a gentle, "Ah, there's my old friend, the judging mind." You can take a breath in and watch that breath go out. You might turn inward to see where the judging is manifesting as contraction in your body. You might then ask yourself the first question of The Work, Is this judgment true?

As a way of assessing the second question of The Work, Can I be absolutely sure my judgment is true? Byron Katie suggests probing a bit further: And whose business is this judgment? Katie teaches that there are three possible answers to this inquiry: it's your business, someone else's business, or God's business. Quite often, you'll find that the judgment in your mind is *not* your business. Discerning what action might best be taken in the face of a challenge *is* your business, but judging is not. This discovery is freeing in itself. If judging is not your business, then you can drop it!

Mindfulness of thoughts and feelings can reveal just how often you are busy with someone else's business, whether with their words or appearance or actions. And mindfulness can also show how monumentally unhelpful this preoccupation is. When the judging mind is active, ask yourself the third question of The Work: How do I react when I think this judging thought? Consider: What is the effect on me? How do I treat the person I'm judging? When judging, do I become tight, cold, superior, and sometimes anxious about whether I'm showing how critical I feel? Do I begin to feel separate from others and sometimes lonely?

Then you can move to the fourth question of The Work: Who would I be without this judging thought? When you ask this question, you may find that, without the judging thought, you're more relaxed, open, friendly—in short, a happier camper. You might drop the ancient habit of trying to be in control of the world. Why continue down this judging path if the effect on others and on yourself is suffering, and dropping the story of judgment is liberating?

The Work is a practical way to put into action Jesus's liberating words to his disciples, "Do not judge, and you will not be judged. Do not condemn, and you will not be condemned. Forgive, and you will be forgiven" (Luke 6:37). When we clear judgment away from the lens of the projector, we know for ourselves the freedom of nonjudgment, of forgiveness. It's a blessed relief.

The Judging Mind Goes on Retreat

One morning on an insight meditation retreat, during a time when teachers routinely invite questions or comments about our practice, I noticed that the judging mind had hooked me again. One participant on the retreat had offered *yet again* a many-worded comment, and his observations were not to my liking. He was taking up too much time, I thought, with not very valuable talk. In fact, it was more than just the length of his observations—it was more that his whole way of being was not to my liking! There was, in my judgment, something wrong with him, this "other" person. Hello, my old friend, the judging mind, once again making someone else "other," making a world of me versus him.

This seemed a good time to do The Work with my judging mind. I asked myself, is it true that this person is taking too much time? *Well, it sure seems that way to me!* And whose business is this? *Actually, not mine. His talking is his business.* What's the effect of this judging thought on me? *Well, I'm getting tight around the neck and shoulders and grumbling in the mind.* Who would I be without this judging thought? *In fact, I'd be just sitting here and noticing how the sunlight is making lovely patterns on the wood floor of the meditation hall.*

Before I asked these questions, the judging mind had me in a tightly focused trance of what was wrong with *him*, the other person. Then, while locked in the judging trance, I had another, secondary judgment about what was wrong with *me* for judging the other person. Perhaps you, too, know how the judging mind likes to pile on, judging your own judgments.

This, of course, is the way the judging mind works. The judgment of a rejected or disallowed part of myself (the part that would take up "too much time") is like an arrow, shot away and projected upon the other. For those of us with strong monitors of the discrepancy between what we want reality to be and what is, it feels natural to find ourselves judging, that's just what our minds do. Judging is a powerful habit-energy, but its energy is destructive only when it operates in automatic, mindless fashion. When judging is held mindfully, its very force can be used in the service of waking up and liberating ourselves. To paraphrase the Venerable Ajahn Chah, judging can lead to more judging—or it can lead to the end of judging and freedom.

After I had asked myself the questions of The Work, I felt an internal shift, a lightening within. The questions served to stop my judging mind in its customary tracks. Instead of thinking that the other person was taking up too much time, a turn-around, "My judging mind is taking up too much airtime!" seemed far truer. Turnarounds are not themselves judgments, but reversals of the original judgment that often result in a humorous "aha!" With this turnaround, it was as though I had cleared the lens of the projecting mechanism and now was getting a very different take on the same scene. I was taking back the projection.

No longer was my gaze narrowly trained only on the other I had been judging. I now noticed how all this drama in my mind had been playing out on the stage of a very lovely rural retreat setting, to which I had been blind during this siege of the judging mind. Hawks, deer, and wild turkeys were literally within my field of vision, a delightful, cooling breeze was blowing, but I, for all intents and purposes, might as well have been in a body bag. I woke up to see that while I'd been looking at the other through the pinhole of my judgment a whole big world was out there.

In the bigger view that followed doing The Work, the other person now dropped into the larger physical spaciousness around us, of which we were both a part. He and I were now two parts among many, the mind no longer deleting out the rest of the picture because it had put the other in the bull's eye of the judgment scope.

Albert Einstein wrote of the panoramic sense of the whole that comes into view when we are freed of what he called the "optical delusion" of separate self and other. When we experience ourselves as separate from the whole, "this delusion is a kind of prison for us, restricting us to our personal desires and to affection for a few persons nearest to us. Our task must be to free ourselves from this prison by widening our circle of compassion to embrace all living creatures and the whole of nature in its beauty."

When we question our judging thoughts, they drop into the spacious ground of awareness. When we drop the thoughts and the stories of the judging mind, we can find freedom. As one Tibetan teacher puts it, "Look. See. Let go. Be free." Similarly, one of the Desert Fathers, Abba Poemen, once asked Abba Joseph, "How can I become a monk?" Abba Joseph replied, "If you want to find rest here and hereafter, say in every occasion, 'Who am I?' and do not judge anyone."

The way to freedom from suffering is captured in this simple saying from Christian tradition. When we drop the judging mind that divides the world into self and other, the mind's natural freedom and compassion appear. When we stop asking, what's wrong with them? and, what's wrong with me? we surrender the divine prerogative, leaving the business of judgment to God. Until we question the judging mind, however, no matter how still and silent we may be on the outside, the judging mind will keep things stirred up on the inside. As Abba Poemen observed, "There is one sort of person who seems to be silent, but inwardly criticizes other people. Such a person is really talking all the time. Another may talk from morning till night, but says only what is meaningful, and so keeps silence."

The silence of the heart, inner stillness, and freedom from suffering begin with awareness of the not-silence and not-stillness and not-freedom of thoughts, especially those of the judging mind. Seng-ts'an, (the Third Zen Patriarch), once wrote, "Step aside from all thinking, and there is nowhere you can't go."

Doing The Work is a way to "step aside." When we stop refusing the suffering in our thoughts and question these thoughts instead, they can be the door to freedom. As long as we are trying to figure out the *why* of suffering, we are distracted from coming to terms with the more important *what* of suffering.

When people are hurting, they do not need explanations of *why;* they are living the *what* of suffering and need someone to help absorb their suffering, to help them cope. They need relief. Whether we can change the external circumstances or not, we can step aside from the stories we tell ourselves about how things and people *should* be, and step into the freedom to take responsibility for our inner landscape, our thoughts about *what is,* and respond out of compassionate awareness. On the difficult path from resistance (Why is this happening?) to acceptance (How can I live with this?), it is a blessed relief to know what helps, and what doesn't.

Blessed Relief: The Work

The next time you become aware that you are judging someone, instead of letting the judgment bring suffering, give yourself a chance to turn things around by practicing The Work:

> Begin by writing down all the thoughts that your judging mind has come up with. Then begin your inquiry using the four questions of The Work.
>
> 1. Ask yourself, are these judging thoughts true?
>
> 2. Can I absolutely know that they are true?
>
> 3. How do I react when I think these thoughts?
>
> 4. Who or what would I be without the thoughts?

Here's an example of what this exercise might look like in real life. Suppose you are particularly annoyed by a colleague, Jack. You would start by writing down all the complaints you have about him. For example, you might write, "I'm angry with Jack because he's a know-it-all who never shuts up and always dismisses my ideas. I wish he would wire his jaws shut and listen for once. He's such a controlling, dominating person. I never want to have to be in a meeting with him again."

You would then take each of these thoughts about Jack to inquiry. It's especially helpful to write down your responses to each question:

> 1. Is it true that Jack shouldn't be such a controlling dominating person? *Well, I certainly experience him as controlling; maybe others do or don't, but I sure do.* Yet even if everyone

experiences him this way, is it true that Jack shouldn't be this way? *I might prefer it otherwise, but the reality is that he is this way.* Is this true that Jack shouldn't be the way he is? If your answer is "no," skip to the third question. If you're not yet at "no," go to the second question.

2. Can I absolutely know that Jack shouldn't be a controlling, dominating person? Can I really know what is best for Jack or for me in the long run? Whose business is Jack's behavior, anyway? Is it my business, Jack's business, or God's business? *Well, I can't absolutely know that Jack shouldn't be this way. Anyway, it's not my business the way Jack is— it's his business.*

3. How do I react when I think this thought about Jack? *Well, I get tight in the face and my eyes narrow into slits with hate-rays coming out. I want to strangle him. I gossip about Jack when he's out of the room. I make excuses to avoid being in his presence. I keep quiet until I can't stand it anymore, then I try to puncture his insufferable pomposity. I find myself reaching for the candy during meetings with him. He reminds me of all the other blowhards I have ever known and of my contempt for all of them.* Can I find a stress-free reason to keep thinking these thoughts about Jack? *Well, no.* Are there any payoffs I get for holding on to these thoughts? *Well, maybe that I get to be superior to Jack.* And what's the effect of this posture of superiority on me and other people? *Well, my significant other tells me it's not such a great effect.*

4. Who or what would I be without this thought about Jack? *If I were unable to think these thoughts about Jack, I'd relax. I'd stop fighting with him in my mind. My body would be like a net and his energies would just blow*

through the empty places but not stick inside the net. If I didn't believe this thought, I'd let Jack be Jack and not judge him. I might even be friendly to him. I might even ask for his opinion rather than resisting him all the time. If I close my eyes and picture him without my story about him, I see a guy who looks fearful and insecure. Without my story about him, I'm more the person I would like to be, understanding and compassionate.

After "judging your neighbor" and asking these four questions, the last phase of The Work is to take your thoughts, turn them around, and see what *is* true. Here are some examples of turnarounds you might make:

- Turn the thought that "Jack shouldn't be a controlling, dominating person" into its opposite: "Jack *should* be a controlling, dominating person." Which seems more true? What, in fact, is reality in this instance? That he *should* or *shouldn't* be the way he is? However I would like him to be, he is the way he is. That's reality.

- Turn the thought that "Jack shouldn't be a controlling, dominating person" into "*I* shouldn't be a controlling dominating person." Hmmm, this is challenging! Could this statement about Jack be just as true about me? Maybe I'm not as overtly, visibly controlling as Jack, but I'm playing the covert control game in demanding that he be different than he is. So, let's see, I want Jack not to be controlling, something that I, myself, have trouble with? I want *him* to change, but I'm fine the way I am? (This is a good time to know Zen teacher Cheri Huber's first rule of projection: What you see is who you are. Or, as the 12-step people say, "If you spot it, you got it.")

- Turn the thought into "*My thinking* shouldn't be so controlling and dominating." Bull's eye. If the shoe fits....

- The ultimate turnaround is when, rather than dreading being in Jack's presence, you say to yourself, "I *look forward* to being in Jack's presence." Why? Because Jack is just the teacher I need to reveal where I'm in contention with reality, where I'm hooked. (As Katie writes, "Remember, beyond the appearance of who it is you are looking at, it is always God disguised, standing in front of you so that you can know yourself.")

As you write down your answers to the questions and the turnarounds, you may find laughter spilling out of you. Sometimes it's a gut-busting laughter that comes as a huge release upon dropping the insanity of your thinking. Sometimes it is of the "oh, my God, I never saw this before and it was right in front of my face" variety. In this case, the laughter is like watching Archie Bunker being unmasked by Edith, only it's you unmasking yourself. Of course, with more challenging examples than the one above, the turnaround may not lead to laughter, but doing The Work will lead to insight and emotional freedom.

3

BEYOND BELIEF

I'm not very much interested in beautiful buildings. What really interests me is how you train your mind.

THE DALAI LAMA, SPEAKING AT
WESTMINSTER ABBEY

A Happy Accident

The phone doesn't usually ring during my morning meditation unless it's a family member calling, and sure enough, it was my then sixteen-year-old son, Alex, who had just left for school.

"Hey, Dad, I've had a wreck. Nobody's hurt, but the cars are pretty messed up."

I told him I'd be right over. I noticed on my way to the accident that I was speeding a bit, and I slowed my car down, lest I have a wreck going to the wreck. But, internally, I was still racing—my heart thumping, my mind cranking out thoughts. I felt reassured that Alex and the other driver were okay, but following a short moment of gratitude quickly came the thought, "This is going to be a big pain in the butt." I was resisting what I imagined was going to unfold.

Nearing the scene of the accident and the already snarled traffic at the intersection, my mind was spinning out variations on the theme of my believed thought, my basic presumption that this was going to be a big pain. For starters, the car that Alex was driving didn't even belong to him; it was his grandfather's. And

my first sight of the two cars did nothing to assuage my presumption. The cars were as advertised: The entire right side of
Alex's car was destroyed, and the other car looked like an accor-
dion squeezed from the front bumper backward. Both airbags in
the other car had deployed, and it was clearly ready for the great
junkyard in the sky. Indeed, this was looking like a very *big* pain.
I found myself dreading standing out on the public thoroughfare
with people rubbernecking to gawk at us. I could already hear
the angry honking of impatient drivers ringing in the air.

As I pulled my car off the road, something in me asked the
Byron Katie question, who or what would I be without the
believed thought that this is going to be a big pain? This actually
was not a random question. I'd been putting this question to
thoughts that would arise around everyday events for some time.
As various thoughts would come to mind, I'd dig a little deeper
into each one, asking myself, who or what would I be without
this thought? Almost invariably a lightening and opening would
follow the asking of this question. It was not so much that I got
an answer but more as if the thinking process itself would stop
for a moment, and as it stopped, a kind of spaciousness between
thoughts would present itself.

At the scene of the accident, when I said to myself, "Without
this believed thought, I would meet this event with spaciousness,"
I experienced the same lightening and opening. Walking over to
Alex, I felt my feet crunching the dry winter grass underfoot. I
seemed to have slowed down internally. I was aware of my breathing in and out. It was good to see Alex unharmed. The other driver,
another teenage boy, looked worried but physically unhurt. I
introduced myself to the police officer and the other boy. After the
ritual exchange of insurance information, I talked with the boy
about his school and where he was planning to go to college.

Alex then replayed the sequence of the accident for me, and
it was apparent he had failed to yield to the oncoming traffic in
making a left-hand turn. As he spoke, I could hear how his mind

had moved into an "if only" line of thinking: if only he had or hadn't done this or that.

After listening to his story, I observed, "Yeah, that's what the mind does after an accident."

Alex asked me, "Dad, what were you doing when I called to tell you about this?"

I told him that I had been meditating.

"Hmm," he said, "I guess I'm lucky."

Indeed, we both were. Whether I'd have asked what my believed thought was had I not been meditating before his call, I can't know. But questioning my thought surely took me into a different space when I arrived at the scene of the accident. In fact, with this simple question, the automatic, anxious energies of resistance arising in me just dropped away. I stopped being in contention with what was going on. There was a wreck. People were honking. Police lights were flashing. I wasn't demanding that it be otherwise. Surprisingly, I was only mildly self-conscious standing out on the road. I resisted the impulse to wave to those scowling motorists who needed to signal that they had been delayed on their morning errands.

I told Alex that a mere thirty-eight years previously, I, too, had a wreck on this very same street just one traffic signal further on, that he came from a noble lineage of wrecks on this road. We shared a laugh of father-son imperfection. It was a nice moment. The wrecker hauled the chariots away from the intersection, and we headed off to the original destination, school, having had our first class of the day in the school of life.

In *Emotional Alchemy,* psychotherapist and teacher on the synthesis of Buddhism and psychotherapy Tara Bennett-Goleman outlines a series of ten believed thoughts that cause a great deal of suffering:

    1. Abandonment: "I will be left."

    2. Deprivation: "My needs won't be met."

3. Subjugation: "It's always your way, never mine."

4. Mistrust: "I don't trust you."

5. Defectiveness: "I'm not loveable."

6. Exclusion: "I don't belong."

7. Vulnerability: "Something bad is going to happen."

8. Failure: "I'm not good enough."

9. Perfectionism: "I have to be perfect."

10. Entitlement: "Rules don't apply to me."

Whenever one of these thoughts arises, it likely carries with it emotional suffering: fear, anger, resentment, shame, sadness, or suspiciousness. I remember once showing this list of thoughts to a psychotherapy client. He looked it over, smiled to himself, and said, "Yep, I'd say all these apply to me." Whether *all* these thoughts apply to you or not, you will likely recognize at least several as familiar companions. Unexamined, these believed thoughts cause a lot of suffering. But when you can hold these thoughts in mindful awareness, you are on your way to discovering a blessed relief, beyond belief.

Spacious Awareness

Zen teacher Ezra Bayda tells of a time when he had become quite discouraged and full of self-doubt. When he went to see his teacher, Joko Beck, to tell her what was going on, she asked him what his believed thoughts were. He realized that he didn't know, that he hadn't bothered to note them. She also asked him if he could reside in the physical experience of his emotional state. In *Being Zen*, Bayda recounts his experience:

For the next few days, whenever the discouragement or anxiety arose, I'd first ask myself what my most believed thoughts were. As they became clear, I would label them: "Having a believed thought: nothing matters." "Having a believed thought: I'll never be any good at this." "Having a believed thought: what's the use?" Often I would have to label the same thought over and over. But once the story line was obvious, it became easier to approach the physical experience of the emotion itself. There was still resistance to the unpleasant quality of the physical experience, especially the physical sensations of doom and anxiety in my midsection. But as I continued to bring awareness to my bodily experience, the density of the emotion began to change. Instead of something solid, the emotion began to break up into smaller aggregates of labeled thoughts and individual, constantly changing sensations....

Through the practice of experiencing, we could still feel some anxiety but not *be* anxious. We identify not so much with "me" or "my anxiety" but with the wider container of awareness.... From this increased spaciousness, there is a stillness within which we can experience what's going on.... We stop identifying with this narrow sense of "self" and start identifying with the wider and more spacious context of awareness itself.

It was this larger, spacious awareness that became available to me on the morning of Alex's accident when I asked, What is my believed thought? Who or what would I be without that thought? It was only when I asked these questions that I could get "beyond belief," beyond my personality with its agendas for security and control. It was only then that my view of Alex's accident could shift from the narrow, suffering frame of mind (What a big pain!) to a more expansive, observing frame of mind.

What surprised me was how the effect of asking these questions rippled through the rest of the day. Approaching the police officer, I found him understanding and helpful, with a wry, experienced humor about the events unfolding, nonetheless imparting

a sense of gravity to the young drivers. At the end of the experience, he said to the boys, "Have a better day."

Later in the day there was another surprise: the insurance
representatives were uniformly competent and kind—not the
experience I expected. But most remarkable was the other driver's mother, who was far more concerned about the safety of
both boys than about the fact that my son was at fault and that
she was clearly inconvenienced and concerned about replacing a
car. "We're Christians," she said, "and we believe that blame
never helps and that understanding and forgiveness do." She
went on to tell me that her brother had recently been terribly
injured by a drunk driver, and she was just grateful the boys
were okay. I told her how moved I was by her generosity.

The experience did not turn out to be a pain—far from it. In
fact, it is closer to the truth to say that my faith in humanity was
a bit restored through the whole event. There were kind, helpful,
generous people in the world. Later, when I shared the episode
with three good friends with whom I meet monthly in a spiritual
friends group, one of them observed how carrying negative expec-
tations into a situation often becomes a self-fulfilling prophecy,
how being "loaded for bear" results in the bear chasing your butt
up a tree—which the bear, of course, can climb. Another of the
group noted that Alex was damn sure lucky I had been meditating! When his own daughter had been in a similar situation, she
had burst into tears when she saw "the look" on her father's face.

You may be familiar with the commercial in which one person witnesses a spontaneous act of kindness and, inspired by
what she has seen, does something kind for someone else. Then
another person is inspired by her kind act and, in turn, helps
another, creating an ever-continuing chain of acts of kindness.
As I made my way through the day after the accident, I noticed
a chain of what Buddhists call *metta*—thoughts of lovingkindness—coming to mind. Thoughts for the other driver and for his
mother and her brother, for the police officer, for the driver of

the wrecker, for the insurance agents: "May you be free from suffering. May you be happy." I found myself wishing each of them
well and found myself, much to my surprise, happy.

Do these wishes or prayers of lovingkindness have an effect
on external reality? I don't have the answer, but I do know that
saying these phrases inclines my own mind toward kindness
rather than judgment, toward openness to possibility rather
than demanding expectation. And that, I think, is the point of
the practice of asking, What is my believed thought, and who or
what would I be without it? That is the point of wishing others
well. These practices open the fearful heart. And when the fearful heart opens, its natural capacities for kindness, compassion,
joy, and equanimity arise. Happiness arises, a happiness not ultimately dependent on outward circumstances. Questioning
believed thoughts is an antidote to suffering that has *already*
arisen, and repeating phrases of lovingkindness is an antidote to
suffering *before* it ever arises.

Incline Your Mind

The Buddha said that whatever we frequently think and ponder
upon, that will be the inclination of the mind as we meet the circumstances of life. St. Paul likewise invited his readers to consider the inclination of the mind: "Whatever is true, whatever is
honorable, whatever is just, whatever is pleasing ... think about
these things" (Philippians 4:8). By making wise choices about
how we incline our minds, we can meet the moment in ways that
decrease suffering and increase happiness.

I was once working with a client who was caught in a maze
of worry, anger, and sadness during his divorce. I suggested to him
that when we're anxious or worried, it can be especially useful to
ask, what is my believed thought? who or what would I be without this thought? My client began to practice asking these questions, but the same thoughts kept arising, seemingly without end.

Then one day he came to his session looking much lighter and reported that he had made a significant discovery. In the midst of a round of worry, he recalled that I had suggested he might choose to incline his mind toward something that might bring him genuine happiness, even in the midst of all his suffering.

He is a person who loves the outdoors, especially hiking and canoeing in wilderness areas. He thought of canoeing the Lewis and Clark route up the Missouri River, and even though this idea made no practical sense to him, he began to plan a trip. He noticed his spirits rising and found that when he actually booked the trip, it was as though his view had lifted from the floor of self-pity and blaming others, and now was looking into an open sky. The simple act of questioning his thoughts and inclining his mind moved him from demanding that his life be other than it was, and he was able to open himself to previously unseen possibilities.

Phillip Moffitt, one of the teachers at Spirit Rock Meditation Center, highlights the difference in the mind between expectation and possibility. In *Dancing with Life*, Phillip points out that expectation is full of believed thoughts that *constrict* the mind into grasping for what is wanted or pushing away what is feared. Possibility, on the other hand, *opens* the mind into spacious awareness of the present moment and into not knowing about the future. When we incline the mind away from the believed thoughts of expectation and toward the sacred now of possibility, we find ourselves standing on what we may discover to be holy ground.

The morning after Alex's accident, I was walking down the driveway to get the newspaper. It was still dark, and a wild, eerie wind was blowing. Rushing along, I noticed a whiff of fear involuntarily arising from I knew not where and, with it, a contraction in my throat. Maybe the fear was a response to the strange energy of the wind. I asked who or what I would be without this fear. In the unknowing following the question, something in me began to slow down. I felt each step, alert to the sound and movement of the wind in the darkness. Something larger than fear now seemed to be present.

A Native American saying came to mind: behold, I am walking on the earth in a sacred manner. With a simple question, what had at first seemed fearful had opened into the sacred now. No longer merely going to get the morning paper, I now walked on the earth in a sacred manner. It was as if the wind had carried the noise of fear away and left an inner silence in its path. I came to a full stop and, savoring this moment, felt happiness arise. I gave an inward bow to the wild, strange, and now holy wind. A half smile came to my face, and I turned to walk back into the house.

Who's Talking?

Alex's accident occurred while I was on retreat—actually, a home retreat with a teacher named Adyashanti. Before Alex's call came, I had been listening to Adya's *Spontaneous Awakening*, a set of recorded talks from one of his teaching retreats. I'd first heard of Adya from a friend at Spirit Rock Meditation Center who had recommended that I go hear Adya when he came to Nashville to give a public talk. I had put his visit on my calendar, begun to read his books, and found his written work fresh and direct. When I heard him teach in person, I found him wise, funny, and non-self-promoting. While he was familiar with and drew upon the teachings of both the Buddha and the Christ, Adya did not locate himself in any particular spiritual lineage. I found this most unusual. Who was this guy, I wondered?

After having given himself to thirteen years of vigorous Zen practice, Stephen Gray, as he was then known, began to question his thoughts, or as he puts it, to find out for himself what was really true. He found that by sitting in silence and not manipulating his mind in any way through specific spiritual practices, stillness naturally arose. His spiritual practice really took off, however, with what he calls "Inquiry," a process through which he began to question his thoughts. He would start with a certain naiveté, asking the basic question, who or what is having this believed thought?

Adya teaches that each of us is a bagful of believed thoughts—who I think I am, who I think you are, what I believe life is all about—and even just one believed thought is enough to cloud the mind. The thought itself is actually harmless; our *attachment* to the thought, *believing* the thought, is what clouds the natural clarity of the mind. It is our identification with the tangle of our believed thoughts that creates suffering for us.

Adya's practice of Inquiry doesn't tell us what to do about specific problems. Instead, we learn to stop asking *what* to do and start asking, *who* is asking? We discover how to probe what is behind our thoughts by asking questions, such as, who is it that suffers? what owns this mind that is in turmoil? what is it that is asking how do I do this or that? Because these questions don't really have conceptual answers, they lead us into silence. They lead us into the mystery of who we truly are, what Adya calls "the nothing behind this dog and pony show called me."

Conventionally, we see ourselves, the *me*, as a *something*, a collection of physical and mental characteristics. Inquiry is a way to see the *me* we take ourselves to be from a very different perspective. With mindfulness practice in general, and with Inquiry in particular, we come to know that there is something beyond our usual ego orientation, that there is more to us than who we usually take ourselves to be. But in order to discover this *more*, we need to learn a way to detach from our thoughts so that these limited thoughts do not define us.

I recently came back from retreat to the usual pile of mail, voicemails, e-mails, and impending work obligations. I diligently worked through the mound of communications, thinking to myself, "This is manageable." But when some large and unexpected pieces of work came my way, I found myself feeling like an overwhelmed air traffic controller. There were too many planes up in the air, and I was never going to get them all on the ground without a fireball. At least this was my believed thought. Accompanying this thought of "too much work," I felt my heart rate increase and my neck become tense. It seemed a good moment to question my believed thought that I had too much work and that I was never going to get it all done. (Sound familiar? Perhaps you, too, have some experience with these believed thoughts.)

I asked myself, who or what is believing this thought that there is too much work to get done? *The one who wants to be productive and get things done.*

And who or what is that? *The one who feels good when he can get things done.*

And who or what is that?

It was with this last question that my mind stopped. I simply did not have an answer to that one. I did not know. And in that not knowing, the tension lifted from my neck, my body spontaneously took a deep breath, and I stepped back into a bigger view. It was not at all true, this story I'd been telling myself. Disaster would not happen if I did not get this work done. My sense of emergency was entirely self-generated; there was no external pressure at all. In fact, it occurred to me that I'd done plenty of work that day, and this believed thought was a signal that it was time for a break. So I called it a day, went to the gym and worked out, and started work the next morning refreshed, no longer believing my thoughts about what *had* to get done.

I once saw a scanning electron microscope image of Velcro that showed in powerful magnification thousands of little hooks reaching out in every direction, ready to fasten tightly onto any nearby loops. I think of my storehouse of believed thoughts as something like that Velcro. My thought that I had too much work to do was just one little hook in a forest of largely unseen believed thoughts ready to attach themselves to multiple loops of suffering. Could it be, as Adya puts it, that there is no such thing as a true belief?

The Cloud of Unknowing

When Adya first started his Inquiry practice, whenever a burning question arose for him, he would write what he himself knew to be true about it, not what any spiritual authority told him. He would write until his knowledge ran out, and then sit at the edge of not knowing. My experience was much as Adya described his own in *Emptiness Dancing*: "Half of the practice of spiritual inquiry is to take you to silence instantly. When you inquire, 'Who am I?' if you are honest, you'll notice that it takes you right back to silence instantly. The brain doesn't have the answer, so all of a sudden there is silence."

As I began to use the method of Inquiry to probe my believed thoughts—what story am I telling about myself? what is noticing? what is thinking this thought? what is feeling this feeling?—each question seemed to take me right into the heart of what one medieval English mystic called "the cloud of unknowing," a space where the mind becomes remarkably still. Many years ago when I read the fourteenth-century spiritual work *The Cloud of Unknowing*, I was left largely mystified as to what the anonymous author could possibly be talking about. It wasn't until Father Basil Pennington at St. Joseph's Abbey and Father Thomas Keating at St. Benedict's Monastery introduced me to the practice of centering prayer, a modern presentation of the method outlined in *The Cloud of Unknowing*, that I was able to discover the sanctuary of silence and stillness and the gifts within this cloud of unknowing.

After years of training in a prayer life that was largely about *saying* something, some words or thoughts or feelings, it was a blessed relief to come to this practice in the Christian tradition that was rooted in silence. I came to know for myself what Jesus promised: "Come to me, all you who are weary and carrying heavy burdens, and I will give you rest" (Matthew 11:28).

While a sanctuary of silence and stillness sounds appealing, unknowing is not at first a comfortable place for most of us. As adults, we are so sure we *know*—or, alternately, so *unsure* we know—that we demand knowing and certainty to stave off the insecurity of not knowing. Knowing is something we think we need to get, yet all of our efforts to "get" whatever we are seeking only ensure that we will not find it. Unknowing, on the other hand, is hidden in plain sight.

The Korean Zen teacher Seung Sahn Sunim famously says, "Only have don't-know mind.... This don't-know mind cuts off all thinking and is the true quiet mind." In the knowing mind are *my* thoughts and *my* opinions and *my* agendas, lots of movement and action and noise. In the don't-know mind, the identification of *me* with the believed thought stops, if only for a moment. Inquiry deconstructs the *me* who wants to know, to get somewhere, to get something. Inquiry helps us to recognize our believed thoughts and to question them, to notice what is *not* thinking, and to let go of thoughts; it drops us into the spacious awareness of unknowing.

Whenever I get caught in the undertow of my believed thoughts, especially thoughts of needing to do things perfectly, I know it's time for some gentle questioning: Who, or even better, *what* is searching? What is judging? What is thinking? What is seeking approval? What wants to be special? What loves? What is fearful? What is not enough? What is happy? What is delighted?

When I ask these questions to my *body,* and not just my head, I sometimes experience energy currents running down my spine and through my body. It feels as if something is waking up within, some tangle is unwinding and unbinding from deep inside. When I question my thoughts and rest in unknowing, the movement of these energies gives me the feeling that something is being rewired within. I can only say that when I tell the truth about what is happening in any given moment, instead of telling myself some story or believed thought about what is happening, these bodily energies begin to manifest as if to say, "Pay attention. This is true."

To awaken is a very simple thing. Waking up is *not believing* our thoughts and our judgments. It is not about adding something or getting something. Instead, it is a remembrance of who we really are. It is not an attainment but a letting go into an unknowing beyond thought and judgment. It is not a getting, but a dropping away—a dropping away of thought and story line.

Awakening can come in all shapes and sizes, at the most unexpected times. On the day of Alex's accident, when I questioned my believed thought that Alex's wreck was going to be a big pain, a little awakening happened and the day unfolded differently than it would have had I continued believing my thought.

Suffering is a tangle of thoughts, feelings, and bodily holdings that can begin to unwind and unbind when we turn and ask, who or what is suffering? When we keep asking until we don't get any more answers, until we enter the cloud of unknowing, we can surrender our searching and rest in awareness itself. A world of possibilities opens up. Even a teenager's wreck may turn out to be a teaching.

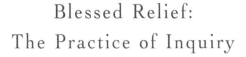

Blessed Relief:
The Practice of Inquiry

Take another look at Tara Bennett-Goleman's list of believed thoughts that can cause suffering:

1. Abandonment: "I will be left."
2. Deprivation: "My needs won't be met."
3. Subjugation: "It's always your way, never mine."
4. Mistrust: "I don't trust you."
5. Defectiveness: "I'm not loveable."
6. Exclusion: "I don't belong."
7. Vulnerability: "Something bad is going to happen."
8. Failure: "I'm not good enough."
9. Perfectionism: "I have to be perfect."
10. Entitlement: "Rules don't apply to me."

Do any of these believed thoughts sound familiar? Choose one thought that seems to keep popping up for you and ask yourself, who or what is believing this thought?

For instance, you might have the thought, "Something bad is going to happen." When you inquire into who or what is believing this thought, you might realize, *the one who has been hurt so many times before.* Then ask, who or what is the one who has been hurt so many times before? Keep inquiring into who or what is believing each thought until you truly do not know.

When you come into unknowing, let yourself rest. Take a breath in, and then watch as the out-breath drops out of your body. As you rest in the rhythm of your breathing, for just this moment, let go of seeking or fixing. Notice what it feels like in your body to let go of your believed thought. Let yourself rest in spacious awareness.

Your believed thought may return many times. Each time it appears is an opportunity for Inquiry. Even though you think you know the answer to your question, inquire again by asking who or what is believing this thought until, once again, you come into unknowing. Each time, make contact with how your body feels as you surrender your thought. Notice how your body feels when you rest in spacious awareness.

4

QUIET AMBITION

We try so hard to hang on to the teachings and "get it," but actually the truth sinks in like rain into very hard earth. The rain is very gentle and we soften up slowly at our own speed. But when that happens, something has fundamentally changed in us.

PEMA CHÖDRÖN, *Start Where You Are*

Not Enough

On the opening night of my first insight meditation retreat, one of the teachers, Phillip Moffitt, asked those gathered, "Why are you here? *Something* brought you here. What was it? Name it to yourself, and as best you can, be thankful for it."

At Phillip's invitation, I found myself wondering what *had* brought me to this retreat. Certainly it was the opportunity to be with Phillip Moffitt and Tara Brach, both Buddhist teachers in the *vipassana* tradition whose writing I admired. And it was the setting of the retreat, north of Charlottesville, Virginia, with a view of the Blue Ridge Mountains and the Shenandoah Valley beyond, a land that had felt like home since the first time I saw it.

But most of all, in a way I could not have fully appreciated beforehand, the chance to deal with a particular kind of suffering had drawn me to this retreat. Thirty years before, I had come this way to college in Virginia, and it was here that I had first become aware of an underground stream of quiet ambition in my life: the ambition to be seen, to be noticed, to be approved, to be recognized. This ambition flowed in part from what I believe is a need we all have to contribute and serve and give in a way that is individually, uniquely authentic. It was during college that I had begun to wake up, by fits and starts, to this passion in myself and to look for ways that I might contribute to life.

Driving past the place where I had gone to college and onto the grounds of the retreat center, I was flooded with memories and found myself asking a not-uncommon middle-aged question. Looking back to my younger self from where I now stood, I wondered, "Have I done enough, been enough in my life?" Embedded in this question was an uneasy sense that I had not, especially compared to others who I imagined had "made it." As a therapist and priest, I knew enough from listening to others how deceiving the appearance of "making it" could be, but in the fantasies of my comparing mind on this day, a familiar story line of suffering emerged: a familiar, believed thought of not being enough. In fact, it was Tara Brach's exploration of this particular form of human suffering in her book *Radical Acceptance* that had most powerfully drawn me to this retreat.

This stream of quiet ambition had run underground in my life because I had been schooled from boyhood not to be too obvious about what I most wanted. Being overtly ambitious was seen as bad form, and I feared being judged if I appeared too obviously determined. Above ground, in my conscious awareness, was the all-too-familiar fear of not being good enough or not measuring up. But below ground my ambition as a teenager was to "make it" in such a way that my insecurities would be swept away by the impressiveness of my accomplishments.

When I went to college, the possibilities for recognition grew and my desires began to match the possibilities. At that time I had no awareness that all the recognition in the world would not quiet my fears of inadequacy. I only knew that I liked the good feeling that came with recognition, and once I'd felt that rush a few times, I was hooked. Someone once said that if you really want others to know who you are, you'll tell them about your addictions. So, here is mine: "My name is Gordon, and I'm a recognition junkie."

The engine of this desire for recognition pulled along with it a train of accompanying fantasies of awards and applause. I know that I am hardly alone in having these thoughts. In *Let Your Life Speak*, writer and teacher Parker Palmer acknowledges that, in young adulthood, he developed "a taste for the prizes" as outward signs of his success. In his *Confessions*, St. Augustine disclosed his youthful wish to have his name burn with approval on the tongues of others. I, too, wished others would think well of me—actually, it was more that I wanted them to think I was *great* and spread the word. Running alongside these daytime fantasies of recognition, however, were nightmares of public embarrassment and failure.

When I was a rookie Episcopal priest, I had a recurring dream of not being able to find my vestments. Often in the dream I was searching frantically to find my sermon and prayer book as the church service is beginning. Mine is by no means a unique clergy dream; many of my ordained priest friends have told me of similar dreams. Over many years as this dream has evolved, I have found in subsequent renditions that I do not, in fact, have to find my vestments. In newer versions of the dream, I can speak publicly without my clerical outfit or the lifeline of my sermon notes or prayer book to keep me from falling into the abyss of my fear of failure. In real-life experience, I have acquired confidence about public speaking and an ability to manage my insecurities. Nonetheless, the underground stream of quiet ambition has kept flowing all the while.

I've now experienced over thirty years of ordained life. Along the way, I've come to know what Buddhists call the Eight Vicissitudes: pleasure and pain, gain and loss, praise and blame, recognition and disgrace. My nightmares about the pain of failure, loss, and disgrace, were expressions of fear, to be sure. But in another, strange way, maybe they were also expressions of my desires—desires for liberation from my addiction, for freedom from the burden of the inner demand for recognition—because my experiences of failure had a way of revealing my addiction in a way that success never did.

Paradoxically, failure brought with it the first flashes of freedom from the addiction. I had to come to know what the Reformation scholar Roland Bainton once called "the failure of success, and the success of failure." I knew that the "successful priest" persona was not the solution to my desire for recognition or a workable cover for my long-standing fear of exposure and humiliation.

It would be some years later, however, before I would come to appreciate the distinction between being *recognized* and being *seen and known*. Grasping for recognition is both a defense against and an obstacle to being truly seen. It is about performance, what sociologist Erving Goffman calls "impression management," a *covering* of what is true. The addiction of recognition always requires another hit, another fix. While I found momentary relief in having my hunger for recognition met, in time it would gnaw at me again.

Intimacy, on the other hand, is a *revealing*, a disclosure of the truth. Interestingly, the Greek word for *truth* used in the New Testament is *aletheia*, which literally means "not covering." Truth, at its most basic level, is "not covering"; it is being known, being real.

I remember a psychotherapy client who had a secret she felt she could never share. She believed that if she allowed anyone to see into her secret, she would be revealed in all her awful not-enoughness. But when she uncovered the truth of her life, first to me, then to her husband, she found relief from decades of suffering. Amazingly to her, this single uncovering delivered her from *all* her fears of not being enough and into a freedom she never imagined possible.

Being seen and truly known goes beyond performance. It has more to do with disclosure and the willingness to allow someone else to "into-me-see"—intimacy. I've come to know that recognition is a kind of fool's gold, while intimacy is the true coin of the realm of spiritual practice—intimacy first with myself, with those who are my daily companions, and as the heart opens in ever-widening circles, with all beings and the Source of life.

Among the tribes of northern Natal in South Africa, the greeting *sawu bona* ("I see you") is the equivalent of *hello*. The proper verbal response in their culture is *sikkhona* ("I am here"). In my life, the desire to be seen and known has run parallel to my fear of being judged and found inadequate. At any given moment, either the desire or the fear might be more dominant. To be judged is to be unseen. And to be unseen is to be anxious, awkward, and vigilant. The freedom to be seen is the freedom to be able to reveal the "I" who is here, to relax, and to receive another's response without trying to control it.

Kind Attention

Before the retreat in Virginia began, I spent some time outside doing qigong with my wife, Kathy, facing the Blue Ridge Mountains in the distance. A rabbit stopped to watch, then hopped away. A shower of oak leaves fell in the autumn wind. Geese passed above and disappeared into low clouds. The afternoon was exquisitely pleasant.

Moments on retreat are not always so.

The first day on an insight meditation retreat is almost always an experience of the Buddha's teaching of the First Noble Truth: there is suffering. The suffering of the aching body sitting cross-legged on a cushion, the suffering of the restless mind

jumping from one thought to another, the suffering of the judging mind pointing out what's wrong. After our first day, Tara
Brach commented, "Eighty-five percent of us are wondering
why we came, if we should leave, or are planning to leave." This
certainly got a laugh of recognition from the group. Later in a
dharma talk, Phillip Moffitt referenced T. S. Eliot's "undisci-
plined squads of emotion" as something we were likely experiencing. Phillip went on to draw a verbal picture of a *New Yorker*
cartoon: a man on the street waving a paper with the headline,
"My issues, my issues!"

My first issue and big aggravation on the retreat was my
reactivity to the three other men with whom I was sharing a
room—and the inevitable tensions of sharing a small space.
Phillip wryly observed that we naturally have a preference for
the pleasant over the unpleasant, and then noted, "That's not our
problem." Our problem, he said, is that we so quickly grasp for
and cling to what we want. The issue is not, is your mind calm?
The issue is, is your intention to keep coming back to what is
happening now? This is the essence of mindfulness practice:
What is happening now? What is *this … now*?

When I'm trying to meditate, often the *this* is that I'm
falling asleep. Tara gave me some practical advice about sleepiness in meditation: focus on the bodily sensation of the in-
breath, then with the out-breath imagine the body dissolving
into the surrounding space.

When I tried what she suggested, it worked. Alertness
arrived, to my amazement, and as I later told her, "It got quiet in
there."

"That's *samadhi*," she said. "That's concentration."

Our practice on this retreat was to meditate in silence for
forty-five minutes at a time. I found that concentration was present in some sittings, but distraction or sleepiness was present in
others. I was learning that I was not in charge of what happened
in any given meditation period, but that I could choose how to

respond. Tara's teaching was helpful: "When you're sleepy during a sitting, you can stand; standing is a fine posture for meditation." And I found that it was. It's a little harder to fall asleep
standing up.

As the week unfolded, more and more I found myself dropping into a large inner stillness, the Great Silence where sounds,
breath, and thoughts come and go, where silence is the *cantus
firmus* beneath all the notes sounding in the mind stream.

One evening, outside the meditation hall after the final sitting of the day, the Milky Way was visible. I felt as though my
body were effortlessly being breathed, and this Great Breath was
breathing all things together into being. The whippoorwills
called. In the Great Silence the stars moved. Nothing was missing. Gratitude spontaneously arose. In that moment, I felt no
striving, no ambition in me—just deep peace. "The peace that
passes all understanding," as Christians call it. How remarkable.

Later, of course, ambition arose again. As Buddhist teachers regularly observe, nothing is permanent, everything changes.
Even as I thought, "How nice ... no striving," a new ambition
arose: the desire to "get it right" in the meditation, the wish for
something special to happen, something like what I had read
about in books, even the Big E—Enlightenment.

This grasping for perfection and singular experiences, this
comparing myself to how I imagined others were doing—this was
nothing new. The retreat was just another stage for the same old
play. What *was* new was how I was learning to relate to the arising of ambition. As I was learning from Tara and Phillip, ambition
is a mind state, one that can be held with kind attention.

This realization was nothing short of a revelation to me.

A particular rainy day on the retreat brought back memories
of loneliness from my first year in college. When memories like
that arose in meditation, I began to be able to hold them with
compassion, with kindness. Later in the night, the hard rain gave
way to a clear sky. The next morning, in the early darkness, the

bright moon was reflected in my mug of tea. As dawn came up, the first sitting of the day was very quiet. I found that I could hold everything without and within in a field of compassion: rain ... wind ... clearing sky ... bright moon ... steaming tea ... each breath ... the others sitting in the meditation hall ... the eggs at breakfast. Soothing tears of gratitude came for the blessings of my life: for my son, Alex; for my wife, Kathy; for our dog, Morgan; for our friends; for this practice.

I found myself silently asking about the preferences and aversions coming down my mind stream, So, what do I have against mud ... sleepiness ... snoring ... grasping ... the desire to be admired ... superiority ... inferiority ... judging ... planning ... grouchiness ... wanting things to be other than they are? If I could hold each mind moment with awareness and kindness, each thought was an opportunity to come into the great field of compassion. Breathing in, "ambition"; breathing out, "kindness."

Spontaneous Joy

One retreat afternoon, Kathy and I ran into each other on a walk down to the river. Silken seeds were flying, dispersing themselves all about us in the wind. We kept the retreat's rule of silence and refrained from asking each other, "How's it going for you?" We walked together in quiet and wandered into a patch of butterfly bushes where hundreds of butterflies were gathered. The scene was pure magic. Down by the river, the sun lit up the water, and autumn leaves floated unhurriedly past. Something was slowing inside me. And from that slowing, joy came shyly peeking out. When suffering is relieved, joy spontaneously arises.

Insight meditation retreats are held in silence, but every other day, you get to check in with one of the teachers for fifteen minutes to talk about your practice and how the retreat is going for you. In one of these check-ins, Phillip asked me about my religious background. After listening to the broad-brush outline of my journey, he said that he found the symbols of Christianity alive but the Western churches in a season of dying. He went on to say that through their symbols, they would eventually be reborn.

I have my own sense of what Phillip was expressing. My aversion to the dogmatic divisions among various Christian factions, the hijacking of religious rhetoric for partisan political purposes, and the downright deadness of much of institutional church life sometimes wears me out. What I was finding on this retreat was a blessed relief from the Christian culture wars.

But there is something still alive for me in the Christian way: the music and devotion, the richness of Christian symbol in the liturgy, the legacy of Christian service, and the tradition of contemplative prayer. Interestingly, on this Buddhist retreat, I was finding the inner realities of heart and mind, of which the Christian tradition speaks, alive and well: mercy, lovingkindness, bearing with suffering, forgiveness, and most of all, compassion. What was present for me—and what seems to be missing in many Christian precincts—is a working knowledge about how to transform, and not merely endure, suffering in its mental, emotional, and physical varieties.

Every night following the last sitting of the day, candles lit up the statue of Kwan Yin, the feminine bodhisattva of compassion, and an image of Sakyamuni Buddha seated under the bodhi tree, one hand touching the earth. The great Christian image of the suffering servant hanging on the tree of life came to mind. As we softly chanted together, I was reminded of hymns to the Virgin in the candlelit darkness of Christian monasteries I have visited. It all felt most familiar to me, the quiet devotion of these Buddhist practitioners. Yet instead of the familiar chants I was used to from the Psalms, we were chanting from the Heart Sutra: *Gate, gate, paragate, parasamgate bodhi svaha!*

As Thich Nhat Hanh explains in *The Heart of Understanding,* *gate* means "gone," gone from suffering to liberation, gone from forgetfulness to mindfulness, gone from duality into non-duality. *Gate, gate* means "gone, gone." *Paragate* means "gone all the way to the other shore of liberation." Gone, gone, gone all the way over. *Parasamgate* means "everyone gone," the *sangha*, the entire community of beings, everyone gone over to the other shore. *Bodhi* means "the light within," "enlightenment," or "awakening." And *svaha* is a cry of joy or excitement, like "Welcome!" or "Hallelujah!" Gone, gone, all the way gone, everyone gone, awakening ... hallelujah!

I noted that my mind was comparing Christian and Buddhist retreat experiences. Comparing, I was beginning to realize, is just one of the things that minds do. But mindfulness of comparing invites the energy of comparing to drop into the background. When this happens, silence arises and quiet dawns in the mind. While mental contents themselves may be pleasant, unpleasant, or neutral, the *awareness* of these contents is invariably something beyond pleasant or unpleasant. The awareness is spacious and peaceful.

At the end of the retreat, Kathy and I took the slow roads home, driving down the Blue Ridge Parkway at a leisurely pace. In fact, we were so slowed down, we rarely got close to the speed limit of thirty-five miles per hour. Over the course of the week on retreat, our lives had naturally slowed down to a human pace. It was a blessed relief not trying to get anywhere other than where we were. What a joy.

The Hungry Ghost

Someone once said that one of the devil's favorite disguises is to dress as a priest in a cassock. There's a lot of psychological wisdom in that nugget. Quiet ambition can take on a variety of forms, and one of them is what the Tibetan teacher Chögyam Trungpa calls "spiritual materialism," the tendency of the grasping mind to make goals in spiritual practice as something else to be acquired.

My own quiet ambition has taken the form of becoming a priest (check), becoming a therapist (check), teaching meditation (check), having articles published (check), writing a book (check). Each of these forms of ambition has brought both satisfaction and frustration, which belong to each other like night and day, up and down. Whether satisfying or frustrating, eventually the light began to dawn on me that none of this business of getting "the check" beside the ambition—spiritual, material, or otherwise—will do it for me. As Buddhist writer Carolyn Rose Gimian says, "You can get all the power and all the material things, you can get all the therapy, you can get all the religion, you can get all the bliss, and eventually it will not be enough."

I have to admit that there is a certain set-apartness that comes with the priestly role, a set-apartness that I have feared and fought and enjoyed. I've quietly enjoyed the distinction, the standing out, but I have also feared and fought the separation that comes with the role. But whatever distinction may come with the role, it does not bring enduring satisfaction. It is not enough; it does not satisfy ambition's Hungry Ghost.

The Hungry Ghost in Buddhist lore is a being that has a huge belly and a tiny mouth and throat. With its enormous appetite and small intake channel, the Hungry Ghost can get only a bit of satisfaction in its tiny mouth in any one bite. Meanwhile, its belly cries out for more and more, so it can never get enough. The image of the Hungry Ghost powerfully conveys what it's like to be condemned to endless, fruitless wanting and grasping—the condition of craving and grasping that the Buddha diagnosed as what ails us.

More is what the Hungry Ghost of ambition—spiritual or otherwise—calls for. Mindfulness has given me a way to recognize this quiet ambition of reaching out for *more* as an old friend. When ambition has me in its grasp, I am pushing and striving and seeking more—more knowledge, more security, more recognition. But when I hold ambition in simple awareness, I *become the awareness* of the energy of ambition. When I hold ambition in the larger field of awareness, the knots of energy in my body that are tied up with ambition's grasping begin to untie. I know this is so because when I tell myself, without judgment, the simple truth—that this is a moment of ambition—I can feel energetic currents begin to move within my body. It *feels* as if something is being untied. Quiet ambition is giving way to quiet awakening.

In a collection of dharma talks, *Sweet Zen,* Cheri Huber explains that the Buddha likened an individual life to a long silk scarf with a series of knots tied in it. The knots represent our conditioned habits, the ways we cause ourselves to suffer. We come to spiritual practice, she says, when our scarves are so knotted there is no room for another knot. Spiritual practice unties those knots, and the experience we gain each time we untie a knot gives us the encouragement we need to take on the next one. In time, we can approach the whole process of knot untying with confidence, lightness, and, increasingly, gratitude even for the knots.

I think of what Phillip Moffitt said at the beginning of this particular insight meditation retreat: "Whatever brought you here, as best you can, be thankful for it." Real healing takes place whenever we can be thankful for the sufferings that have brought us to the gate of liberation.

By the close of the retreat, I felt grateful for my learning: I now understood that ambition, whenever it quietly takes birth in me, invites me to pay attention, to hold it in awareness. Later in my Buddhist training I would learn to look within and inquire, who or what is ambitious? But at least I now knew that by holding ambition in mindfulness, in kind attention, I could untie one more knot on the scarf. I understood that when the craving for distinction dropped away, I could know a quiet awakening of joy that no distinction could ever bring, a peace that passes all understanding.

Blessed Relief:
The Sacred Breath

When you notice that the demands of ambition—or any other form of grasping—cause contraction in your mind or body, pause and bring attention to your breathing. This exercise in mindfulness of the Sacred Breath is a first step in being able to experience the *desire* of ambition without suffering from the *demand* that you get what you want. The Sacred Breath loosens your identification with any particular mind state and opens you to dimensions of yourself *beyond* the suffering of getting or not getting your desires met. This Sacred Breath practice is especially powerful when you are looking out on a vista, but you can undertake it wherever you are.

- Take a moment to position yourself where you can see outside. Be aware of sounds … and sensations in your hands … and the coming and going of your breathing.…

- With your eyes open, on the in-breath, draw your gaze to an object close to you. As if you were watching the tide coming into the shore, let your awareness of the in-breath draw your vision close in. On the out-breath, let your gaze move out into the distance. As the tide of the breath flows out, allow your vision to drop into the distance.

- As you continue to follow this tidal rhythm of the breath, let your body be an open gate through which the breath of life is moving. If it is comfortable for you, let your gaze swing in and out to the rhythm of the breath. Or, if it is more comfortable, rest your gaze in the middle distance, not focusing on any object in particular, but on empty space while feeling the flow of the Sacred Breath. In time, you may wish to close your eyes, softly noting the in and out of the breath with a mental "In" and "Out." On each out-breath, let your body dissolve into space.

5

AN INSTRUMENT OF PEACE

There was one monk in the monastery who really irritated me.
I couldn't bear him. Just at the sound of his voice I would feel
aversion arising in my mind. I asked Ajahn Chah what to do,
and he said, "Ah, that monk is very good for you. He's your
real friend. All those nice friends, those other bhikkhus
[monks] that you get on so well with, they aren't very good for
you. It's that one who is really going to help you."
AJAHN SUMEDHO, *The Mind and the Way:*
Buddhist Reflections on Life

Angr-r-r-y

As children are wont to do with their parents, my son, Alex, once
instructed me in the uses of anger—when he was but three years
old. A houseguest was staying with our family for several days,
and my son, at their first encounter, engaged this man with
openheartedness and the full range of his little boy enthusiasms.
Our guest, a big, sturdy, sixty-year-old man, initially was
charmed by the attentions of this small whirlwind around his
feet, but during the second day of his stay, his response changed.

Alex's mother and I began to notice that our guest would correct Alex in what felt to us a heavy-handed fashion. He would
engage Alex in physical "play" that was too rough even for this child
who delighted in roughhousing. Our guest seemed to enjoy pushing
Alex beyond the limits of fun into distress, then minimizing Alex's

protest or upset by saying, "That's not hurting you." At this point, either my wife or I would intervene, breaking up the battle between the three-year-old and the sixty-year-old.

As the visit wore on, I got increasingly angry at the way our guest was attempting to control, correct, and intrude upon our son. Yet I was feeling stuck in the tension between wanting to protect Alex and wishing to avoid conflict with our guest. When our guest told us he had straightened out his own children with the back of his hand, we got the hint, and I responded with a cold silence.

Finally, things came to a head. Our guest was "teasing" Alex again, calling him a "rascal." There wasn't any humor in this name-calling, only an attempt to needle. I was about to intervene, ostensibly on Alex's behalf but also out of my own mounting resentment, when Alex took care of the matter himself. Drawing his small body up to his full forty inches, Alex got into his antagonist's face and angrily said, "My name isn't rascal! My name is Alex!"

There followed a moment of silence in which all present knew that the balance of power had shifted. Alex's mother and I exchanged a glance of a certain satisfaction. The teasing and the bullying stopped for the moment.

For Alex, anger was simply a part of life. Each night as he went to bed, his mother and I engaged in a three-question ritual, asking him, "What made you happy today? What made you sad? What made you angry?" He loved to ask both of us the same questions, and it was sometimes challenging to reply in a way that was truthful and comprehensible to him. He especially enjoyed asking us the last question, growling like a lion as he said the word *angr-r-r-y*.

Alex could hardly have known how much he was helping me by asking the question in such a playful way. Learning how to be with myself when I am angry at myself, how to be with others toward whom I feel anger, how to be with others who are angry with me—these struggles have been a growing edge for me for a number years.

Both Jesus and the Buddha were models of nonviolence toward self and others, and they have much to teach about handling and caring for our anger. In Buddhist thought, mindfulness of feelings is the first step of dealing with anger, a process of *self-soothing* that gives us time and space to be with our anger before it becomes destructive. Christians have many models and examples for the next step in handling anger, *self-defining*, which stops demanding something from others and starts taking personal responsibility. The third step in handling conflict, *self-transcending*, takes us beyond anger and blame and opens us to new possibilities in relating to others and to ourselves.

Self-soothing, self-defining, and self-transcending are the antithesis of the "get it out of your system" school for dealing with anger. As Father Thomas Keating points out in *Invitation to Love*, we need to recognize that our anger is our own, triggered but not created by another's actions. Anger often arises out of threats to our wishes for security, affection, or control. Life offers us regular challenges to these wishes, and unless we develop ways of holding the vulnerabilities underneath our anger in loving awareness, we will surely find ourselves controlled by anger when we feel threatened.

Self-Soothing: Bringing Attentiveness to Anger

The well-known prayer of St. Francis of Assisi begins, "Lord, make us instruments of your peace. Where there is hatred, let us sow love." The prayer continues with a series of antitheses: where there is injury/let us sow pardon, where there is discord/union, doubt/faith, despair/hope, darkness/light, sadness/joy. If we read these antitheses in an either/or fashion, they would seem to suggest that our task as instruments of peace is not to feel or express hatred, doubt, despair, or sadness, but to suppress our feelings and enact their opposites. But if we read these antitheses in a both/and fashion, a different meaning emerges: the path to authentic love goes directly *through* hatred, the path to authentic union *through* discord, the path to ease *through* unease. This understanding suggests that the spiritual life is not an uprooting of our emotional unease but an attending to it so the kingdom of peace can be cultivated. This second understanding is truer to my own experience.

Practically speaking, I have found that suppressed anger has an unfortunate way of leaking out sideways in sarcasm, indirect expression through bodily tension and dis-ease, or direct explosion in aggression. My attempts to uproot negativity haven't worked. There is, however, a way of feeling and expressing irritation or frustration that goes beyond denial, surrender, or retaliation. This way employs not suppression but mindful attentiveness to anger, a willingness to wait and watch with anger until discerning what action, if any, to take.

This capacity for simple attentiveness to our anger is foundational to the skillful handling of emotions, for without mindfulness, we cannot begin to discern what to do with our anger or any other emotion. Before we *do* anything with anger, we must learn how to *be* with it. Thomas Merton, in *The Wisdom of the Desert,* relates this story told by the Desert Fathers:

> A brother asked one of the elders: What is humility?
> The elder answered him: To do good to those who do evil to you.
> The brother asked: Supposing a man cannot go that far, what should he do?
> The elder replied: Let him get away from them and keep his mouth shut.

It is easy to misinterpret this exchange as an invitation to conflict avoidance, but it is my experience that restraint is, in fact, the first step to conflict resolution. Whenever my heart rate rises in the face of provocation, I do well to wire my jaws shut. Nothing good ever comes from responding when I am in the midst of an emotional hijacking. Later, when I have gotten hold of *myself* and not, as I might want, the throat of the person provoking me, I have a better chance of transforming the energies of anger into something useful and nondestructive. This is the practice of what Buddhists call "the way of nonharming," what St. Francis called "becoming an instrument of peace." If we practice this "custody of the tongue," as the Desert Fathers and Mothers named it, we can develop the capacity to attend to our anger before we visit it on someone else. Even if we have well-practiced habits of verbal hostility, we can learn another, nonharming way, actually rewiring the brain as we learn this new way.

It turns out that the old adage "think before you speak" is more than just good advice. In *Emotional Alchemy,* Tara Bennett-Goleman describes recent discoveries by Dr. Richard Davidson at the University of Wisconsin, who has found that mindfulness practices activate the left prefrontal area of the brain, dampening negative feelings and generating positive feelings. Let's say you have a disturbing experience. Immediately, your amygdala, a structure deep in the emotional brain, sends out a surge of messages. If you engage in mindfulness, you actually strengthen the neural pathways that tone down these messages, inhibiting an automatic, "mindless" response.

In other words, if we first keep our mouths shut, we might then figure out if and how we should open our mouths about our anger. The first step is simple, gentle attentiveness to our anger. This capacity is not something that develops overnight, but it can grow out of what the early Christian monks called *ascesis,* or "practice."

It was Thich Nhat Hanh who first taught me how to hold anger in all its varieties (irritation, frustration, blame, boredom, rage, hatred, revenge) within the kind awareness of self-soothing.

This poet, peace activist, and Zen master was once nominated by Dr. Martin Luther King Jr. for the Nobel Peace Prize. To see him slowly and mindfully walk or drink a cup of tea or speak is to see real presence and peacefulness incarnate. His compassion and disciplined spiritual practice come together in such a concentrated, powerfully embodied way that Jim Forest of the Fellowship of Reconciliation once called him "a cross between a caterpillar and a bulldozer."

Thich Nhat Hanh has tasted the bitter fruit of violence in his native Vietnam and has dedicated his life to helping people discover the path to peace. Thây, as his students call him, offers retreats to Vietnam veterans in our country to teach them mindfulness of feelings. He tells of one American commander who had lost over four hundred of his men in a single battle on a single day and, for twenty years, had been unable to get past his anger at the useless loss of these lives. Another man had taken the lives of children in a Vietnamese village out of anger and revenge and, after that time, had lost all his peace. He could not even sit alone in a room with children.

In his work with veterans, Thây begins with a basic mindfulness practice: Look after your feeling. Don't try to suppress it or drive it out. Simply watch it in an affectionate and caring way by naming it and watching your breath come and go. In *Peace Is Every Step*, which is essentially a manual in how to become an instrument of peace, Thây writes:

> When we are angry, we are not usually inclined to return to ourselves. We want to think about the person who is making us angry, to think about his hateful aspects: his rudeness, dishonesty, cruelty … and so on. The more we think about him, listen to him, or look at him, the more our anger flares. His dishonesty and hatefulness may be real, imaginary, or exaggerated, but in fact the root of the problem is the anger itself, and we have to come back

and look first of all inside ourselves.... Like a fireman, we
have to pour water on the blaze first and not waste time
looking for the one who set the house on fire. "Breathing
in, I know that I am angry. Breathing out, I know that I
must put all my energy into caring for my anger."

This idea of caring for anger is very different from visiting it
upon someone or hoarding it in bitterness. You start by simply
noting the presence of anger. You don't make any attempt to tell
the story of what brought about this mind state, but instead simply name your mind state with a soft mental note: this is anger.
It's helpful to think of mental noting as a kind of mirror. When a
figure (anger) appears before the mirror, the glass faithfully
reflects the image without judging it in any way. Mental noting
means letting go of analyzing in favor of just noting what is taking place.

    This practice of mindfulness of feelings is the first step in
caring for ourselves when we're caught in a storm of reactivity.
By practicing this means of self-soothing, we can not only prevent the emotional storm from growing in intensity, but we open
up the possibility of transforming anger into peace by giving
ourselves time and space to embrace our anger.

Self-Defining: Being Willing to Speak Your Truth

One year after Easter, I made a ten-day retreat with Father
Thomas Keating at St. Benedict's Monastery in Snowmass,
Colorado, to deepen my practice of centering prayer. The fifteen of us on the retreat had been forewarned that there were
no single rooms and that our accommodations might offer a
certain lack of privacy. I had anticipated having a roommate,
but I had not imagined one who suffered from sleep apnea. I'd
never before shared a room with anyone who suffered from

this malady, but I've since resolved, as best I am able, never to do so again.

Sleep apnea is a breathing pattern in which loud snoring alternates with a long silence of no intake of air. Once my roommate fell asleep our first night, I became all too intimate with the rhythms of sleep apnea. As I lay awake hour after hour at night, the walls fairly shook at the inrush of air past my roommate's tonsils. Then all would fall quiet for an unpredictable time, until a blast of sound signaled the cycle had begun again. After two nights of no sleep, I found myself toying with the hope that, in the long silences between snores, my roommate might actually have died. Alas, he snored on. Several nights into the retreat, I finally began to get some sleep, but my exasperation toward my roommate's snoring was just a warm-up for what was to come.

The retreat itself had a rhythm of silent periods of centering prayer, followed by conferences with Father Thomas, followed by more centering prayer. In the Christian contemplative tradition, the root of interior prayer is silence. While conventionally we may think of prayer as thoughts or feelings expressed in words, this is only one form of prayer. Evagrius Ponticus, a fourth-century Christian teacher, taught a form of "pure prayer" that he described as "the laying aside of thoughts." Following in this tradition, Father Thomas writes in *Open Mind, Open Heart*, "Centering Prayer as a discipline is designed to withdraw our attention from the ordinary flow of thoughts. We tend to identify ourselves with that flow. But there is a deeper part of ourselves ... the inner stream of consciousness which is our participation in God's being."

The method of centering prayer is to sit in silence and let go of every thought that may appear flowing down the stream of consciousness: an emotion, a memory, an image, a plan, even a "spiritual" experience. Whenever you become aware of any thought, you lay it aside by bringing to mind a sacred word, a single word such as *peace, rest, mercy, Jesus,* or *Mary.* This sacred word is a symbol of your intention to rest your awareness on the stream of consciousness itself rather than on the objects or thoughts floating down the stream. When you let go of your thoughts and return to the sacred word, you empty the mind of its customary routines. You consent to open yourself and wait in silence, surrendering your whole being to God.

The practice of centering prayer and Father Thomas's teaching on it was, for me, both encouraging and unsettling. It was encouraging in that I found more genuine vitality in this contemplative prayer form than any Christian teaching I had heard in a long time, but unsettling in that the practice of centering prayer looked dangerously like it might change my life in ways for which I was unprepared. In particular, Father Thomas pointed out how our "false self," with its demands for security, recognition, and control, catches us in the clutches of suffering. Whenever our security is threatened, our hope for appreciation is denied, or our urge for control is frustrated, one of the varieties of anger often arises.

In centering prayer, the instruction is to let go. Let go of your demand that this moment be other than what it is and return to the sacred word. Let go of your demand for security, appreciation, or control. The practice of laying aside thoughts in centering prayer is training in *slowly* dismantling the demands of the false self. Again and again, ever so gently, as you let go of your thought or feeling and return to the sacred word, you cultivate an intention to put yourself at God's disposal.

In the silence of the retreat, in the noise of my roommate's snoring, I had many opportunities to be attentive to my own desires for security, recognition, and control—and the variations of anger bubbling up when those wishes were not met. And I had many opportunities to let go.

A Buddhist monk once described monastic life as "the practice of the one hundred thousand frustrations." This was pretty much my experience on this Christian retreat. Privacy was in

short supply, several people were gifted at getting on my last
nerve, and I, obviously, was not in control. I like being in control.
Life together in close community was not, I was finding, all it
was cracked up to be. The prescribed schedule conspired to dis-
able my usual freedom in arranging my day, and especially
galling to me was the fact that some folks on the retreat honored
the rule of silence more in the breach than the observance. Even
though I had volunteered for this experience, I chafed at the
restrictions.

Who thought it was a good idea to do this retreat, anyway? And who had invited these other people? Wasn't there a
hermitage where I could be by myself? With these questions
my tension mounted, as did my resistance to the retreat. My
neck and shoulders felt as though they were in the grip of a
giant hand. I resisted reality, resisted what was, clung to ideas
of what I wanted, which as the Buddha pointed out, is the
cause of suffering.

Then, a week into the retreat, I had this dream: I am back
home doing some work on my car and I've just taken off one of
the wheels. I go inside my house, only to find when I return that
all four wheels of the car are now off, and the car is resting dis-
abled on its axles. Furious and wondering who might have done
this, I watch a man get off a bus and walk toward me. This man
bears a strong resemblance to Thomas Keating. He acknowledges that he has removed the wheels and, furthermore, that he
has done a bit of rearranging under the hood. I start yelling at
him, attempt to throttle him, and demand to know if he is competent to overhaul my car. Before he can respond, I awake.

Although I was angry in the dream, my tension dissipated
upon waking. As I thought about the significance of the dream,
I realized that Father Thomas and the practice of centering
prayer were messing with my way of "getting around." I had
taken off one of my wheels (by showing up for the retreat), but
Father Thomas had something more radical in mind. His teach-

ing was beginning to rearrange things "under the hood"—in particular, my ways of responding to threats to my security and sources of esteem, as well as my wishes to control others and events.

Following the explosion of anger in the dream, a surprisingly deep sense of peace settled in. Something had shifted internally, and thereafter my resistance to the retreat diminished. I found myself laughing at the uncanny wisdom of the unconscious.

The day after the dream, we had a time to check in with one another to say how the retreat was going for us. When my time to speak came, I observed to the group that we were not keeping the rule of silence, and that unless we negotiated a change with one another, my preference was to maintain the silence at the times prescribed. Some agreed with my preference, others dissented. In the end, we resolved as a group to be more attentive to the rule.

In speaking up, I felt as though I had finally joined the group, had finally shown up for the retreat. Rather than withdrawing from the retreat or retaliating out of irritation, I was able to state aloud my preference about the rule of silence. I was able to self-define. And I was able to do so because of the self-soothing and custody of the tongue that I had practiced during the time of centering prayer.

In the great scheme of things, the snoring and the stretching of the silence rules I experienced were hardly major problems. They were, instead, the everyday irritants of life, merely magnified in the silence of a retreat setting. As you read this, you might well ask, why doesn't he just get over it? I have, in the past, asked myself the same question! But my sense is that what passes for "getting over it" for many of us is often a conflict management strategy of avoidance, denial, or distraction that may, in the short run, appear successful, but in the long run numbs us to our inner and interpersonal life, with fateful consequences.

What often destroys relationships is not so much what is said, though words can certainly be very damaging, but what is not said.

To put it simply, self-defining puts our selves into words: "This is what I think, this is what I feel, this is what I will do, and this is what I won't do." By self-defining, we say who we are. We give up the useless effort to control how another should behave and, instead, take responsibility for the words and actions of the only person for whom we are accountable—ourselves.

Self-defining is what Rosa Parks did when threatened with arrest on a Montgomery bus. She replied simply, "You can do that." But she would not move to the back of the bus. Self-defining is what sixteenth-century theologian Martin Luther did when he declared, "Here I stand. I can do no other." Self-defining is the nonharming willingness to speak your truth, even in the face of intimidation and harm. And in this truth is a powerful presence.

For Christians, Jesus himself is *the* model for self-defining. When he spoke the words, "You have heard it said of old ... but I say to you" (Matthew 5:21), he was saying what he thought, what he felt, what he was going to do, and what he was not going to do. He never returned evil for evil, but he challenged unjust boundaries. In his table fellowship with outcasts, he redefined who was "in" and who was "out." In his cleansing of the temple, he re-drew necessary boundaries, saying, in essence, "I will not allow you to do that here." In forbidding his disciples the use of force at the time of his arrest, he made his most forceful expression of his boundaries: he was willing to go to the cross rather than flee or retaliate. Even more, he bore compassion toward his tormentors, recognizing that, in their ignorance, "they do not know what they are doing" (Luke 24:34).

Being able to self-define was a turning point for me in this retreat; from that moment things got better. As the 12-step folks like to say, "It got better, and it was me." Instead of responding with mounting anger to things I couldn't control, I began using the silence of centering prayer to be attentive to this anger and its coming and going. In the silence, I watched my reflexive, habitual angry responses to perceived threats and frustrated desires, how they arose and receded. I let myself feel the experience of anger in my body: my constricted throat, tightened shoulders, and hardened gaze. I soothed myself by turning attention to the coming and going of my breath. I asked what story I was telling myself about how I or others should be. Most radical, rather than blame others or blame myself for my reactions to them, I did something quite unfamiliar and held my struggles in loving attention. Returning to the sacred word and letting go, I could return to rest in silence, again and again.

This experience was new and different for me at the time. Anger arose, but my need to get rid of it or do something about it diminished over time when I simply sat with it attentively. Through this gentle, accepting attention to my anger, letting it be rather than forcing it away, something in me was getting overhauled.

This would not be the last time "my old friend anger" (Thây's phrase) would come with me on retreat, as following chapters will reveal. The habits of anger and blame do not disappear overnight. As Father Thomas likes to say, the false self doesn't just roll over and die. But when we truly comprehend the suffering our anger brings us, and we hold this suffering in loving awareness, we are on the path to freedom, however distant the final destination of full liberation.

Self-Transcending: Bringing RAIN to Blame

My teacher Tara Brach has been invaluable in bringing together for me the insights of psychology and Buddhist meditation on how to approach what is beneath or behind anger. Whether we are angry at ourselves or someone else, we usually have a story of blame consolidated around a believed thought that somebody is wrong, someone is bad. But underneath that story of blame, there is some point of vulnerability in us, some unmet need, something that wants kind attention. The "trance of blame," as Tara describes it, is our attempt to anesthetize the pain of what lies underneath, to create a false refuge from this underlying pain. When we can be mindful of the energies of blame—in our mind and our body—we can let go of the story of blame, open to the vulnerability underneath, and come out of the trance in which we find ourselves.

Let's say, for example, that you've just learned someone has been gossiping about you, saying some very unkind things that, in your view, badly misrepresent your motives. And now this person is going about publicly besmirching your name. You find yourself feeling outraged. You're thinking how unfair he is, how wrong he is about you, what a *!#@* he is, how you'd like to retaliate by saying a few things about him. Self-righteously, you imagine setting him straight or beating him up, but only after having made him pay by having others think poorly of him. Your believed thought is that, once justice is served, you'll have made him pay and you'll feel better. But, as Tara points out, *justice never heals the wound of loss.*

Instead, thoughts of retribution will generate deeper suffering in you, squeezing out the pleasures of your life. When you are in the grip of blame, you have no relief. Even though you might recognize that you can never feel comfortably at home in your life as long as you are blame-storming, it is still easy to keep fanning the flames of blame. Blame both feeds you and consumes you. You may not even want to stop blaming.

Tara uses the Buddhist image of the two arrows of suffering to explain how blame works. In this example, the first arrow is the shot of physical and emotional pain you feel when you initially learn that someone is gossiping about you. The pain of this wound cannot be avoided; it has already happened. But if you attempt to anesthetize the pain of the first arrow with, of all things, a second arrow—blame—you are taking a false refuge from the rawness of the original wound. You might think you'll feel better by blaming: "My suffering is his fault. If he hadn't gossiped, I wouldn't be feeling this way. He's bad." You may hope to anesthetize the pain, but you actually multiply your suffering. Your blame harms you far more than the person who wounded you. You can make a different choice that will lessen your suffering. You can choose to wake up from the trance of blame. This, Tara says, is a true homecoming, an exile's return from the land of demanding that life be other than it is.

An acronym for this practice that my Buddhist teachers have offered has been hugely helpful to me when I'm caught in the middle of a blame cycle. It is the acronym RAIN, which stands for Recognition, Acceptance, Investigation, and Non-identification. The intention to "bring RAIN to blame," as Tara puts it, is a powerful antidote to the suffering of blaming.

The first step of RAIN is *recognition*, which means simply noting that this is a moment of anger, that anger is like this, in the mind and in the body. It is an observation that you have a mind filled with rage, or at least what Tara calls "uncharitable mental commentary."

The second step, *acceptance*, is a matter of acknowledging that this moment of anger cannot be otherwise. You may not like it, you may want it otherwise, but "it is what it is," and you stop demanding that it be something else. How you recognize and accept the emotion (and your resistance to the emotion) makes all the difference. If you can accept anger with the mental tone of kindness or hospitality, you are practicing compassion. Kindness to the emotion opens the way for it to pass through; fighting it ensures it will hang on like grim death. Joseph Goldstein, in *One Dharma*, suggests thinking of negative thoughts

as Halloween trick-or-treaters who have come to visit in frightening or worrisome or infuriating costumes. We can acknowledge them, invite them into our homes, sit them on our laps, and
allow them to go on their way out the door when they're ready.

Acceptance often comes down to this question: can I simply
be with this emotion and let go of the hope that it will soon
depart? If I am able to do this, spaciousness in which the emotion is simply allowed to be can arise.

The third step, *investigation*, is a shift to curiosity about
your physical and mental experience of this moment of anger.
You check out where you are feeling vulnerable, where the
blame resides in your heart, mind, and body. How do I feel it in
my body? What thoughts am I having right now? What story am
I believing? Can I drop the story line and simply be with the
physical sensations of the emotion? Once you start exploring
what this feeling is like, you've removed your focus from that
"bad" person out there and introduced a new tone to the experience, that of simple curiosity. Noticing where bodily tension
arises, staying with it for a few minutes to watch how it changes,
and attending to the breath at the same time can be especially
helpful.

The fourth part of RAIN, *non-identification*, means just
that: don't identify with the emotion. There is always more to
you than the moment's fear, anger, or sadness. This feeling does
not exhaust the fullness of who you are. Whatever emotion you
are having, it is a cloud that, for the moment, covers the lumi-
nous spaciousness of what the Tibetans call "the sky-like mind,"
or big mind. Small mind is covering big mind. You realize that
this "mind moment" is not *me* or *mine*, but rather an impermanent energy passing through. You see anger not as *my* anger and
personal, but as *the* anger and impersonal, something afflicting
many other persons on the planet. When you can dis-identify
with the feeling, the spaciousness of the big mind can shine
through. Remembering what lies behind the cloud of anger can

be like getting a peek at the blue sky after days of overcast weather.

Non-identification is the essential step in self-transcending. Suffering exists and you are present to it, but there is more to you than your suffering. You can be present to your hurt and vulnerability, but the hurt and vulnerability are not you. And the blame is not you. You are the awareness of the contents of your mind, but you are not exclusively identified with any particular content or wound. You are the consciousness of the emotion and not the emotion itself. And in this awareness, your identification with the emotion dissolves and you transcend the way you conventionally understand yourself.

Go back for a moment to the gossiping example. If you were to put RAIN into practice, the scenario might go something like this. When you first learn of someone gossiping about you, you simply *recognize*, without judgment, your initial flash of anger. You *accept* that multiple causes and conditions have come together to make this moment the way it is; the next moment may be different, but this one cannot be. Then you begin your *investigation:* When you first learned about the gossip, what believed thoughts came with your anger? What needs of yours were not being met—the need to be understood? the need to be treated fairly? the need to be respected? Rather than focusing on what the other person said, you choose to be present to the physical sensations of vulnerability in yourself, to your body's response to not having your needs met. You check it out by asking, what is happening in my body when I tell this story? who would I be and how would my body feel without this story? how long have I felt this way? Does this feel familiar? You allow yourself to feel the "ouch" of the pain without resorting to blaming the one who hurt you.

Finally, you invite *non-identification*. You realize that this anger, even with all its intensity is not *you* or *yours*. You see it as *the* anger, an impermanent energy moving through your mind and body, but not something that defines who you are. You are more than this passing energy. You are the awareness of this energy.

By bringing RAIN to blame, you undermine your story of blame along with its strategy of keeping you from feeling vulnerable. You begin to *feel* your vulnerability, in the body and in the mind. As you hold that vulnerability in mindful, loving presence, it will begin to heal. When you can let go of the story of blame, your healing can begin. You will understand viscerally just how much suffering is hidden under the layers of blame. When you can bring loving presence to that suffering, you can wake up from the trance of blame and come home to yourself. The fruit of this homecoming is known as forgiveness, and it is the very heart of Jesus's teaching.

Jesus's willingness to drink the cup he was given and to bear his own cross with forgiveness marks the self-transcending step in handling anger. Jesus's self-transcending love moved *through* his anguish, his vulnerability, and the anger of others, not *around* them. In the language of theologian Reinhold Niebuhr's Serenity Prayer, "accepting what we cannot change" is a movement of self-transcending. In this surrender, we let go of our own preferences and simply bear reality. We carry what we must without resistance and without blame, not demanding that things be other than what they are. We commit ourselves into the hands of a greater spirit.

A problem for some Christians is making the move to surrender or self-transcending *before* engaging in self-soothing and self-defining. This is a false surrender, a spiritual bypass that often results in passive accommodation to abuse or injustice, or in playing the victim role with the attempt to induce guilt. Not only does this spiritual bypass masquerade as genuine surrender, it also fails to address unfairness and injustice both interpersonally and within the community. This false surrender is *not* an instrument of peace. Only when self-soothing and self-defining have taken place is it truly possible to let go, as Jesus did in his passion, to engage in self-transcending.

We can become instruments of Jesus's peace when we are present to our own anger and that of others, learning with mindfulness to transform the energy of anger into compassion and peace. Self-soothing contains the angry urge to strike back. Self-defining converts the energy of anger into powerful presence. And self-transcending commits us to a loving awareness beyond our personal desires and agendas, surrendering our anger to God's peace and reconciliation. In walking this three-fold path, we find a way through discord to unity, through hatred to love, through injury to pardon. We become instruments of peace.

Blessed Relief:
Working with RAIN

The RAIN acronym is an especially valuable tool in bringing mindfulness to strong emotions. The next time you find yourself in the middle of an emotional hijacking by anger (or another strong emotion, such as sadness or fear), try this RAIN technique to help you see into and through the storm of the emotion to a larger and more spacious awareness.

- **Recognition** When you find yourself on emotional overload, this simple "stop, look, and listen" step is a fundamental place to start. All you need to do is recognize the emotion that you are feeling, to simply acknowledge the anger (or whatever the feeling is). Here is anger—it's just a fact. Try saying to yourself, "Anger is like this ... it's here." The key is to be nonjudgmental and open about what, in fact, is taking place.

- **Acceptance** This is the time to turn your inner critic off. You may not *like* how you feel, but you can acknowledge that it is what it is and you can stop demanding that it be other than it is. Try saying to yourself, "I accept the presence of this anger; I will let it *be* and I will let my resistance to anger *be*." This is the necessary first step in letting go of your emotion's hold on you.

- **Investigation** Here is where it gets interesting. Think of this step as a wide-open invitation for your curiosity. With kind exploration, ask some questions. What is this anger like in my mind? At what exact moment did this anger arise, what triggered it? What thoughts accompany my anger? What is this anger like in my body? Specifically, where does the energy of anger show up in my body? How does the bodily energy of anger change moment to moment? How big is this anger in my body? Is this energy stationary or moving, hot or cold? If it had a color, what color would this energy be? What believed thoughts come with the story of anger? All of these questions are ways to investigate, to witness, to hold your anger without letting it take over you.

- **Non-identification** This is the time to sort out "who's who." Non-identification is a matter of remembering that your feelings are not *you*. A clever way of practicing non-identification is to imagine for a moment that this feeling you are having belongs to someone else. This strategy is a way to temporarily distance yourself from the delusion that you are nothing but this feeling. Most important, let yourself rest in the awareness of the anger. Let the anger be just one mental content flowing down your mind stream. Notice what other contents are also in your mind stream, and recognize that you are more than any passing content. Your anger has come, and gone, and will come again. But your awareness remains.

6

MEETING OUR EDGES

If we go to spiritual community in search of perfect peace, we will inevitably meet failure. But if we understand community as a place to mature our practice of steadiness, patience, and compassion, to become conscious together with others, then we have the fertile soil of awakening. One Korean Zen master told students that their communal practice was like putting potatoes in a pot and spinning them around together long enough to rub off all the peels.

JACK KORNFIELD, *After the Ecstasy, the Laundry*

"You All Belong"

When my teacher Phillip Moffitt asked if I'd be interested in joining a training program for community dharma leaders at Spirit Rock Meditation Center, I felt as if I had won the lottery. I'd already done a number of retreats at Spirit Rock, and I felt a deep connection to both the teaching and the teachers there. Even though Spirit Rock was on the other side of the continent in northern California, it had become a spiritual home away from home. I felt honored to be asked to join this group of ninety people from across the United States, Mexico, Canada, and Britain. I was curious to see how training in Buddha dharma would compare with Christian formation, how the two would be alike and how they would be different, and if there might be Buddhist wisdom that would enrich Christian practice.

The first meeting of the Community Dharma Leader Training was to take place on the East Coast at the Garrison Institute, a former Capuchin monastery across the Hudson River from West Point. Catching the train at Grand Central Station to travel up to Garrison, I found myself excited about what lay ahead.

At Garrison, I discovered that the monastery chapel had been reincarnated as a meditation hall, with a great golden seated Buddha at the visual center. Side-by-side with the original Christian stonework, the imagery stood as a testament to Garrison's new interfaith mission. On a wordless level, I found the transformation of this Catholic house of religious formation into an interfaith retreat center deeply inspiring. The dual spiritual iconography seemed to give outward expression to the inner movement into silence and stillness of my own Christian and Buddhist contemplative journey.

As we introduced ourselves to one another in the opening session, I told the group about my Christian roots and my gratitude for the Christian teachers who first introduced me to the Buddhist path. I went on to say that, because of the open-mindedness of my Christian teachers and the open-heartedness of my Buddhist teachers, I'd come to realize there was no need to excise my Christian heritage to be a part of the Buddhist community, or *sangha*. In fact, I had for some time found the Buddha's teaching breathing new life into my understanding of the gospel of Jesus. In the days to come with this new group, I would find people in this Buddhist *sangha* warmly receptive to the presence of a Christian priest among them. Moreover, a number of them were eager to talk about the full range of their own Christian experiences, from the unsatisfying to the nourishing.

Along with the warm reception and reassuringly familiar feel of the old Christian monastery at Garrison, I felt another, less welcome—though familiar—feeling: a little anxiety at being in a large group of strangers. Part of my own story line has been the thought, "I don't do large groups very well." I knew from my work as a therapist that I am not alone in this feeling. Many, if not most of us, are a bit overwhelmed by socializing in large groups. I also knew that the purpose of this week was not socializing, but the prospect of being in this new group still felt a little scary. Over the years, I've learned to cope with this anxiety by moving toward others and not hanging back, but I couldn't help wondering just how I would belong here. This was probably the most diverse group of people I had ever joined, and we had committed to spending a week together every six months for the next two-and-a-half years. I wondered what I had gotten myself into.

One of our teachers, James Baraz, spoke directly to the anxieties of this new group, knowing that each of us was probably experiencing something similar. He reassured us by saying, "You all belong," and invited us to "keep looking for the good." He then had us break into groups of three, and asked each of us to share something about a time when Buddhist teachings had helped us through a tough period. We got real, quickly. As one person, a former Catholic nun, said after this exercise, "I feel my heart beginning to thaw."

I thought of something Phillip Moffitt had advised at the beginning of another retreat: "Have no expectation; be open to possibility." I very much wanted to be open to the possibility that I might meet my old social anxiety and my story line of "not being enough" in a different way with this group, without expecting any particular outcome. This was a new chance to do some mindfulness practice with my old stories.

As the week unfolded, I met lovely and fascinating people and saw that, indeed, there were all sorts of possibilities for new friendships. Whenever I moved toward someone who seemed different from me in outward style or background, I found the other person quite friendly and receptive. I began to relax.

The Failed Buddhist Bypass

It just so happened when we arrived at Garrison, so did a rare heat wave, with temperatures in the one hundreds. At that time, Garrison had no air conditioning. As the days of relentless heat and humidity wore on, a collective aversion arose to our mutual physical misery. Meditation sessions were sauna-like. Our morning yoga left us dripping with sweat. One of our teachers, Joseph Goldstein, told us this was good practice for life in Burma, should we find ourselves on retreat there. Several of our group had ordained as monks in Thailand and Burma, and they confirmed Joseph's observation. None of this made me want to head to Asia any time soon.

Nonetheless, in spite of the heat, things were going pretty well for me. I was settling in and making friends. As the early days of the retreat passed, I was using the RAIN acronym to be mindful whenever a moment of fear arose around my old story line of shying away from large groups. I came (almost) to relish fear arising because the very act of using RAIN led to my *not* identifying with the fear, and non-identification opened up a surprising new spaciousness. I thought to myself, "Hmm, I'm really getting somewhere with this practice."

I fell into an early morning routine of running, doing qigong while looking out across the Hudson, and then heading inside for yoga with our teacher Jonathan Foust and the first meditation of the day. Given my general happiness, I was blindsided when all of a sudden the heat within the group began to match the heat outside. The tone of our gatherings went from amicable to angry in the blink of an eye. Here's how I remember it.

We had just agreed upon some norms for conversation, what Buddhists call "right speech." As such things go in the life of groups, soon after the norms had been elaborated, they were tested. The testing came around diversity—the experience of being "other"—and the suffering of not belonging. As one presenter said, while the ultimate truth is that we are one, this ultimate truth may fail to do justice to the experience many of us have of not feeling safe in a room with people who don't look like us.

What began as a sharing of the suffering that comes with feeling "other" quickly morphed into charges of insensitivity, racism, and sexism. I heard critical statements made by some who felt excluded. I watched as some who were attacked confessed tearfully to their insensitivity, with promises to try to be more sensitive, while others grew quiet. The rising level of tension seemed beyond the ability of all of us to contain, in spite of our best efforts. Over time, I found aversion to the whole diversity topic arising within me. When I was charged with insensitivity in a small group, I found aversion arising hotly within me. Aversion is simply resistance in all its varieties: hatred, anger, irritation, frustration, avoidance, withdrawal. If grasping has a moving toward quality, aversion has a moving against or moving away from quality.

And when this aversion arose, frankly, I didn't want to practice RAIN with it at all. Even though RAIN had helped me with intense feelings before, my heart wasn't in the practice now; I had no real receptivity to my feelings. And, without the intention to work with the feelings, RAIN is not a magic bullet. By itself, it will not put out the fire of aversion or any other intense feeling.

The weather was unrelentingly hot, and I was boiling inside. I had no desire to drop RAIN on my anger. I was feeling anything but compassionate. I was mad and sick of the heat outside and the heat inside. I more than doubted whether I wanted to be a part of this group. I just wanted to be out of there! This was a moment of big disillusionment, a moment that I came to call "the failed Buddhist bypass." The Buddhists weren't going to give me a pass from conflict any more than the Christians.

Earlier in the retreat, Joseph Goldstein had said, "No matter what the situation, we are responsible for our mind states." Though I knew Joseph was correct, I didn't want to be *mindful* or *responsible* for what was going on in my mind. Instead, I found myself blaming—blaming others at the retreat, blaming the teachers for not somehow protecting us, and, of course, blaming myself for not handling it all better. Hello, my old friends, anger and blame.

"Wait a minute," I said to myself, "I thought the Buddhists would be better behaved than the Christians!" I had seen *way* too much of this drama before: members of religious communities expressing their views in an aggressive way, and others allowing the aggression in the name of "tolerance" and "kindness." Part of my previous enjoyment at being in the Buddhist *sangha* had been the sweet absence of Christian quarrels, a refuge from the self-righteousness of the religious right and left. I found myself thinking, "I'd rather have bamboo shoots shoved under my fingernails than participate in another round of this dance."

Truth to tell, my heart does not leap up at the first sign of a good fight. When I was a rookie priest, I tended to avoid tension and tried to accommodate the wishes of others. I just wanted people to be nice. I came to see in time, however, that my "nice" exterior masked a good deal of hostility. Silent withdrawal and judgment were my true inner responses to conflict. Outwardly compliant, inwardly defiant was my modus operandi. Over a number of years, I have come to see this as a losing strategy, and much of my training as a therapist has worked at this edge, learning to acknowledge my feelings and to respond in ways other than avoiding, accommodating, fleeing, attacking, silently judging, or freezing.

Nonetheless, the eruption of conflict in the community dharma leader group caught me off guard. In retrospect, this was a shattering of the fantasy many of us bring to religious communities, the fantasy that in *this* group, we have finally found the idealized family we've always been looking for, where there is no conflict. The reality is that in life together with *any* group, the question is not whether there will be conflict, but whether we will choose to use the energy of conflict to grow in wisdom and compassion, or to harden in accusation and blame.

One of our group who had worked with prisoners at San Quentin said, "Sometimes I want to belong, and sometimes I don't." This statement beautifully captured my own ambivalent feelings. In spite of James's opening reassurance that we all belonged, once the conflict began to emerge in the group, I wondered both whether I wanted to belong, and whether this group, with its stated intention to act with kindness and compassion, would be able to find a way through its conflict.

The Tibetan teacher Chögyam Trungpa once said that the work of the spiritual life is to meet our edge, and soften. I was meeting my spiritual edge, and hardening. The hostilities expressed in the group and my unverbalized judgments were like flypaper: everything stuck to the aversion hanging in the retreat. Even pleasant moments, such as doing qigong out by the river at dawn, were tainted.

I saw my own attachment, my own grasping to have things the way I wanted them, in this diversity drama: I'm very attached to being treated kindly and to seeing others treated kindly. When I'm not being treated kindly, and when others are not, I can get real cold, freezing up in anger and withdrawal. As the oppressive heat wave hung on, so did my strong aversion to the conflict. A sense of personal failure in handling my anger and doubts about Buddhist mindfulness practice began to arise in me.

When our teacher and group leader Tara Brach reminded us all that fear is the primal mood of the separate self—the self that feels that it doesn't belong—she seemed to be speaking directly to me. Not belonging, feeling "other"—all my fears were in full gear. That night I had a dream that my hand was badly cut and, to my horror, live insects were flying out of the cut. I awoke terrified.

What was I going to do with my disillusionment with the *sangha* and with myself, with the festering hostilities now flying out from inside me? What was I going to do now that the Buddhist bypass around conflict wasn't working?

As I left the retreat, I had little desire to return for further engagements with the group. I thought of something Jonathan, our yoga teacher, had said one morning after a session. Whenever his father, a World War II veteran, encountered an unpleasant experience, he would say, "At least no one is shooting at us." On the train back into New York, I was glad to be away from the verbal shots and so looking forward to getting home. But the weather of the week delivered its own final parting shot when a spectacular thunderstorm shut down LaGuardia Airport before my flight to Nashville could depart.

By the time my flight was finally cancelled, it was midnight. There were no hotel rooms close by and no flight out until the next night. By now I was way past empty. I was feeling full of self-pity. Waiting in line to rebook my flight, I saw a frazzled mother with an infant in a stroller trying to cope with the airport chaos. I asked if I could help her with her baggage. She thanked me but declined in a grateful way. Something softened in me; my gaze opened from its frustrated stare. I recalled a quiet, thoughtful person on the retreat who had observed, "Generosity is easy. Selfing is hard."

Generosity is opening into spaciousness and kindness. The eyes of generosity smile naturally. But "selfing" is contracting in fear and anger. It's narrow and hard and vigilant. There had been a lot of selfing going on in me during the retreat, and I was exhausted from it! As a part of this selfing, doubt had risen up mightily. What if the practices I'd been learning weren't really up to the task when things got hard? What if *I* wasn't up to the task of holding all these intense feelings in spacious awareness? What if mindfulness practices turned out to be a dead end? Even as I asked the questions, I recognized I was suffering what is known in Buddhist circles as a "multiple hindrance attack," when all of the Five Hindrances—grasping and aversion and restlessness and fatigue and doubt—gang up to overwhelm the mind.

I thought of Rick Fields, a former editor of *Yoga Journal,* and his response when he was first diagnosed with cancer. He started taking good care of himself and thought he'd be ready if he had a recurrence. Yet, in spite of his practice and preparation, when his disease did recur, fear and anger arose and completely took him over for a time. He wrote that he felt he had failed and that his practices had failed him. He, too, was flooded with negative feeling, wondering, what has all this lifetime of practice been worth?

Finally, I was able to find a hotel room, but at great distance from the airport. After a good sleep with the blessed relief of air conditioning, I awoke refreshed for the first time in a week. My morning routine of qigong, yoga, and sitting meditation left me feeling re-centered. I was aware of feeling allergic to anything Buddhist, a hindrance hangover from the retreat, but one story from the retreat kept coming to mind.

Tara had told us of the Sukhothai Buddha statue in Thailand, a large, seated image of the Buddha thought to be made of plaster. In 1955 the statue was being moved, but it slipped from its crane and fell into the mud and the plaster cracked. A monk peering into the crack discovered what had been hidden for several centuries: the five-ton statue was solid gold. It was the largest golden Buddha in the world. The statue had been fashioned between the thirteenth and fifteenth centuries, but its true nature had been disguised to prevent Burmese invaders from melting it down. Those who had covered it in plaster had died, and over the years its true identity had been forgotten.

I realized that I had been seeing the plaster, not the gold, on the retreat. In the weeks that followed, I came to see something I hadn't seen before: mindfulness practice isn't about being a Buddhist or Christian, it's about letting go—of attachments, of clinging to the way we want things and people and ourselves to be. In order to let go, we have to keep seeing where we are clinging, where we are wanting what isn't and resisting what is, where we are hooked. When we can begin to accept where we are stuck, the stickiness of our clinging begins to loosen up. The plaster begins to crack. The goodness shines through.

Buddhist teacher Pema Chödrön tellingly observes, "Nothing ever goes away until it has taught us everything it has to teach us." As much as I resisted the thought, I knew I had more to learn about handling conflict and letting go.

Nonviolent Communication

Six months later, I flew to northern California for the second meeting of the group, this time at Spirit Rock Meditation Center. I still wondered if I belonged, but I had the hunch that others were wondering the same thing. Although I was wary, I was willing to be present at this second meeting and I resolved to keep looking for the goodness and gold underneath, in others and in myself. I also knew that Buddhists had methods that could help us metabolize our conflicts, but I wondered whether we as a group would utilize those methods.

On the flight out to Oakland, I read a book that had been assigned to us, *Nonviolent Communication* by Marshall Rosenberg. Rosenberg, a student of the humanistic psychologist Carl Rogers, has made it his life's work to throw himself into the breach of just about every conflict you can imagine: Israel/Palestine, Hutu/Tutsi, labor/management, students/school authorities, nurses/hospital administration, gang versus gang, and family member versus family member.

When I began Rosenberg's book, I was skeptical that any process was going to be able to help our group, and as a know-it-all therapist, I was doubtful that there would be much new to me in the book. I was wrong. As I read *Nonviolent Communication*, I found I was learning a lot, that Rosenberg had some fresh and promising ideas, and I became curious about how this material would play out with our group.

As we reassembled, it was clear there were a number of unhealed wounds from the previous meeting. Some folks, like me, had done their not-belonging quietly, some had done it more verbally and loudly, and some had done it by withdrawing into meditative silence. One person described that first meeting as "pure torture." Whatever our mode of survival, what many of us were able to share was our sense of not belonging.

Into this setting of mutual vigilance and suspicion walked Miki Kashtan, a facilitator from Marshall Rosenberg's Center for Nonviolent Communication. Miki had our attention from the very beginning when she said that she was interested in dissolving the dichotomy between compassion and full honesty. She believed we could learn to be honest with one another, and kind, without withdrawing or attacking. Miki said this even though she knew that we, like all human beings, form at the drop of a hat what she called "enemy images," especially when we see someone as "other," or their behavior as undesirable to us.

Miki explained that Nonviolent Communication (NVC) is a way of empathic listening to feelings and needs, a way of honestly expressing feelings, needs, and requests, and a way of communicating to meet both parties' needs. As she outlined the four-part method of NVC, she assured us the method was simple, but not easy:

1. Observation: noticing what is happening *without evaluation*

2. Feeling: expressing emotions *without an accompanying story or believed thoughts*

3. Needs: naming what is most important to us

4. Requests: saying what we want to meet our needs, *not what we don't want*

NVC begins with *observation,* which simply means reporting on what has been or is happening. Observation is not evaluation but something more akin to what a video camera would record. This first step is an invitation to convert judgments and evaluations into straightforward observations. For example, the thought, "You don't like me," is an evaluation. If you convert this to an observation, you might notice, instead, "You walked into the room without speaking to me."

In response to certain events and observations, *feelings* naturally arise. NVC teaches that it is not another's behavior or outside events but *our* needs that cause our feelings. When our needs are met, we are reasonably happy. When they are not met, we're likely to be dissatisfied. The goal of NVC is to take 100 percent responsibility for our own emotional state. When we express feelings in NVC, we do so simply by naming them, without reference to the story of *why* we are feeling the way we are. Without telling another that "you made me feel" a certain way, we just state the truth of our own feelings: "I noticed you walked into the room without speaking to me, and I felt uneasy."

One of the key assumptions of NVC is that we all have certain universal *needs:* needs for safety, sustenance, understanding, rest and recreation, community, creativity, autonomy, and a need to make our own unique contribution to the life we share together. Actions such as control, domination, blame, and vindication are not needs, but strategies to get needs met. These strategies don't work in the long run because they don't take the needs of the other into account. NVC teaches not only the importance of recognizing our needs but also the importance of making intelligent guesses as to what needs are driving the feelings of the other, no matter how toxic another's behavior. As Marshall Rosenberg says, even when we are misunderstood and mistreated and our own needs are denied, we can use NVC to dig out "the need behind the no" in the other's behavior.

In order to get our needs met, the last step of NVC is to make positive *requests* for specific, constructive, observable behaviors. These are not demands for someone to *stop* doing something, but requests to *begin* a behavior. If there is a hint of guilt, shame, duty, or threat in our request, we have issued a demand, not a request. Demands undermine relationships, while requests let others in on what is most important to us.

NVC was exactly what our group at Spirit Rock needed. Joseph Goldstein had been teaching that we were responsible for our mind states, but we needed a method to show us how we might do that interpersonally when the going got rough in our group. With Miki Kashtan's help, NVC gave us the tools to drop our enemy images of each other, to speak honestly and compassionately. I have never seen a group reorient itself from suspicion and hostility to mutual hospitality and belonging so effectively. Something special was happening, to us as a group and to me. We were discovering together that, for all our diversity, we had at least one thing in common: no one felt they really belonged; everyone felt to some degree like an outsider. When we could name that "not belonging" and own that no one else was doing it to us, things began to open up.

By the end of the second retreat, I found I had wholeheartedly and authentically become a part of the group. I found the teachings on diversity enormously helpful. To my surprise, I found myself mentally noting, "The joy of belonging is like this."

One of our facilitators on the retreat was a physician whose medical practice was in a clinic for the homeless in San Francisco. She knew a lot about how hard it is for human beings to feel safe. She had us sit in two concentric circles, knee-to-knee, facing each other, for a wordless meditation. She invited us to close our eyes and center ourselves with our breathing. Then she asked us to open our eyes and hold each other's gaze while the person in the inside circle made this wish: "May you be safe. May you be protected. May you be free from suffering.

May you be happy." The outside person then returned the wish to the inside person. We closed eyes and let it all sink in, and then moved musical-chair style around the circle to repeat the wish to each person in the group. After this meditation, there was no more talk about not belonging.

All beings have needs to be safe. All of us have needs to belong, to be treated fairly and with respect. When those needs aren't met, there is constriction, bondage, and behavior that can be unskillful, or even harmful. Through NVC and other mindfulness practices, the Spirit Rock Community Dharma Leader Training was giving us a way to be compassionately with "the undesirable," with what we thought didn't belong—in ourselves and in others. What the Buddhists were teaching me is that we can't nurture true community on ideals alone. We need *methods*, such as Nonviolent Communication. The command to love and forgive is not enough. I think of what the theologian Søren Kierkegaard called our need for "training in Christianity." How remarkable that I received this training from the Buddhists.

May the Circle Be Unbroken

Two-and-a-half years after the first retreat at Garrison, when the community dharma leaders met for our last retreat together, we once again experienced a difficult moment. As before, the trigger for our troubles was an exercise around diversity and the experience of exclusion, and the exercise stirred strong feelings in a number of us. But rather than blaming and accusing, this time we did something different.

The day after the exercise, we sat in a large circle with six seats in a smaller inner circle. Any member of the community who wished to speak was invited to take a place in the inner circle. After we shared some silence, those seated in the inner circle began to speak, one at a time, addressing not one another but the community as a whole. After talking, the speaker would listen to another, then vacate his or her seat for someone else who wished to take it.

There were a variety of thoughts and feelings shared, strong feelings and different points of view. Each person spoke with honesty and kindness, and their words were received with respectful attentiveness. There was a profound, spacious silence that held this conversation. Observations were made, feelings shared, needs acknowledged, some requests were made. There was room for all our differences because this time, unlike our first retreat, there was a great field of compassion in which we were holding one another. We had formed bonds of trust and affection, and even though disappointments had been triggered by the exclusion exercise, we cared enough to speak our different truths in love. The room was filled with loving presence and forgiveness. We had come a long way.

There is an old Christian spiritual titled "May the Circle Be Unbroken." This, I think, is a fond hope for many of us in spiritual communities. We hope in our communities of faith to find the ideal family, where we will be understood and received and acknowledged for our contributions. Ideally, the door to the Buddhist *sangha* is an open gate, where no one is excluded. Ideally, at the table Jesus sets, everybody is invited to belong.

In time, however, the realities of life together will inevitably disillusion us of the fantasy of finding the ideal family in any given community—spiritual or otherwise. It is closer to the truth to say that the circle will likely be broken, that people will have their issues with one another. The question for me is not whether there will be misunderstanding, conflict, or injury, but whether we will learn together how to repair the circle when it has been broken. It takes a commitment of spiritual practice to extend a community's reach, in ever-widening circles, so that nothing and no one is left outside.

In Christian communities, we have the model of Jesus repairing the circle of his beloved community. Before his passion, when he broke bread with his disciples, he gave them himself, his own broken body. And he received them just as they were, broken. After his resurrection, he received Thomas's doubt and Peter's shame and Mary Magdalene's longing and wove their broken circle back together with the power of his loving presence and forgiveness. Their circle was not so much unbroken as broken and reformed; in the end, their belonging became stronger for having been broken in the first place.

This, too, was my experience with my dharma sisters and brothers in the circle at Spirit Rock. James Baraz was right from the beginning: we all did belong; we just had to discover this for ourselves.

Blessed Relief:
Nonviolent Communication (NVC)

The practice of Nonviolent Communication can bring about a remarkable change in your way of listening and communicating. NVC will first show you how cluttered your mind and speech might be with evaluation. To begin, commit to practicing NVC for a week and see if you notice changes in the way you hear yourself and hear others. Every time you find yourself making a judgment or an evaluation (whether it is positive or negative), turn it into an *observation,* and then take a look at what you or another may be *feeling* and what *need* drives that feeling. Finally, see if you have a *request* to make for a positive, observable behavior from another. Keep in mind the four steps of NVC:

1. Observation: notice what is happening *without evaluation.*

2. Feeling: express your emotions *without the story or believed thoughts.*

3. Needs: name what is *most important to you.*

4. Requests: say what you want to meet your needs, *not what you don't.* Remember: A request is *not* a demand.

Here's one scenario of how NVC might play out. Say your child has come in from school and immediately dropped all his stuff right in the entryway. The first step of NVC would be to state your *observation* to your child that his gear is on the floor (rather than making the evaluation aloud that his attentiveness to the cleanliness of the house is *deeply* deficient). It might be sufficient for you simply to make this observation; He might then clean up the area without your even requesting that he stow his gear. He might get the hint. Or not.

Assuming you're not so lucky, you move to step two, your *feelings*. NVC teaches that it is not your child's behavior but your need that causes your feeling. So, you might say that you're feeling a little irritated because your need for order isn't being met (as if he didn't already know that you're strongly invested in this picking-up issue).

Let's say your child is involved in a video game with lots of gunfire and is not much motivated to stow his gear on your timetable. Assuming you can get his attention, you might make what Rosenberg calls "an intelligent guess" as to what *his needs* might be. This is very important. "Maybe you're enjoying playing this game right now and have the need to choose the time when you pick this stuff up." Should he nod that you are on target, you might then ask, "How do you think we *both* might get our needs met, yours for freedom to choose and mine for order around home, sweet home?"

Or, you might simply *request* that he stow his gear. "I'd like you to pick this stuff up before dinner in fifteen minutes." Notice there is no hint of a demand.

With a little luck, and the fact that you are not cramming your demand down his throat, perhaps he will collaborate with you on working out a solution. The violence of the video game has, at least, not broadened into the domain of your relationship. This is nonviolent communication.

Whether the issue that arises is inconsequential, as in this example, or there are very large stakes at play, the method is the same. Be patient with yourself. This is not a method you will likely learn overnight. It is also important *not* to attempt NVC in the middle of an emotional hijacking or make a request laced with sarcasm or not-so-subtle demand. When you are speaking from a calmer place, you are more likely to get what you need.

You might give yourself a gift and read Marshall Rosenberg's *Nonviolent Communication* for yourself, visit his website at www.cnvc.org, or arrange to work with someone who has been trained in Nonviolent Communication.

7

BEGINNING ANEW

If you let go a little
You will have a little happiness.
If you let go a lot
You will have a lot of happiness.
If you let go completely
You will be free.

AJAHN CHAH, *A Still Forest Pool*

Unwrapping the Experience

It was the week after Christmas, and a couple was telling me how the holiday had gone for them. I have come to call these counseling sessions that debrief the joys of Christmas "holiday horrors." The couple began by saying their teenage son had wrecked his truck on the Christmas Eve ice on the way home from a family gathering. Following a few minutes behind, they and their daughter had come upon the truck hanging in a ditch. Son was okay; the truck was not. Mom was not at all happy. But, as she'd been practicing, at the scene of the wreck she simply noted her unhappiness to herself. "Mind with anger," she observed silently, and mostly held her tongue. As she was describing this, I silently said to myself, "Progress."

In the past when this mother had become anxious, her anxiety had surfaced not in its true form, but disguised as anger. She now knew this about herself. She also knew that when her voice

was RAISED at the children, her husband would become the
VOICE OF CALM for the family. This was an old, familiar, and
unhappy dance for this couple, each fruitlessly hoping the other
would change. Mom felt unsupported by Dad's so-called equanimity and inability to discipline the children; Dad wished Mom
could get a grip on her hurtful reactivity.

This day, as Mom recounted the event, it was different.
She expressed heartfelt appreciation for her husband's grace
under pressure at the site of the accident and, more remarkably, regret for her angry reactions toward the children in the
past. All three of us knew she came by her angry response
nobly: her own parents were awash in anger during her growing-
up years. We had come to have a lot of room for her habit of
anxiety-to-anger conversion, when the seed of worry would
morph into exasperation and irritation. Today, the room felt full
of warmth and goodwill as she gave voice to her appreciation
and regret. Morgan, my Jack Russell terrier co-therapist, was
curled up in the chair with me. The fountain was gurgling
outside my window.

Dad, on this day, was doing his own share of appreciating
his wife, in particular for how she comforted him when he came
home after midnight, cold and worn out from dealing with the
truck. He had found himself sad that night, and he wasn't sure
why. As we explored the sadness, I learned that he had a tradition of reading "The Night Before Christmas" to his special-
needs child after tucking her into bed on Christmas Eve. On this
night, however, she'd already fallen asleep by the time he arrived
home. Dad felt he had let her down by not making it home
before she'd konked out. But with the wisdom of mothers, Mom
had suggested, "Why don't we go ahead and read to her anyway,"
and so they did. Not deeply asleep, their daughter came wide
awake along about "... not a creature was stirring, not even a ..."
and brought the enthusiasm to the old story that she did each
Christmas. The whole family was first in tears of gratitude for

the joys this child brings to them, then in hysterics as she mimicked her father, "… now Prancer, now Dancer …"

In our session, Dad acknowledged with deep feeling that maybe his sadness had not so much been that his daughter had missed the reading, but that *he* had missed it. Growing up in his family, he said, it was hard to be honest that he was ever disappointed, much less to count on having that feeling validated.

Listening to this couple appreciating each other and acknowledging their regrets, I thought of my teacher Thich Nhat Hanh, and a smile of gratitude came to my face. Several years ago I had been on retreat with him and learned of the practice he calls "Beginning Anew." It was this practice that I was using to help this couple to unwrap their Christmas experiences: the sweet, the sad, and the maddening.

A Place to Begin

One of the most challenging aspects of life together in any relationship or community is getting conflict—and our anxiety about conflict—out into the open where both can be addressed. Private griping, the nursing of grievances, and playing "nice" split people and groups into factions of disenchantment and mutual demonizing. Given the inevitability of conflict in our common life, we need a way to *incorporate* it rather than ignore or avoid it. In essence, we need a time and place to be attentive to conflict and a structured way to invite the negative in along with the positive.

Beginning Anew is a ritual that Thich Nhat Hanh has introduced to his community of Plum Village in the south of France, where he now lives in exile from Vietnam. As part of the weekly rhythm of the *sangha*, time is set aside for people to give voice to their feelings of appreciation, regret, and what Nhat Hanh calls the "negative seeds" of anger, fear, and sadness. The ritual is a way to ensure what Thây terms "good emotional circulation" in a community, and its lineage is ancient: the Buddha prescribed the practice 2,500 years ago for his monks and nuns on the eve of every full moon and new moon.

As Thây describes this ceremony in *Touching Peace,* participants sit in a circle with a simple flower arrangement in the center. After fifteen minutes of silent, mindful breathing, a bell sounds and those present are invited to share what they *appreciate* in each other. The person wishing to speak walks to the flowers, takes the vase in her hands, and returns to her seat. She does not flatter; she speaks the truth. While she is speaking, no one interrupts; she is allowed as much time as she needs. When she is finished, she returns the vase to the center of the room. The bell sounds, and when the group has taken several breaths, someone else who wishes to speak may bring the vase back to his place.

In the second part of the ceremony, participants may express *regrets* for what they have said or done or failed to do. Those listening do not reply or correct or excuse the person speaking; they simply listen, remaining silent throughout. As Thây advises, "Compassionate listening is crucial. We listen with the willingness to relieve the suffering of the other person, not to judge or argue with her. We listen with all our attention." He suggests that those listening follow the rhythm of their breathing to maintain a centered presence and silence that receives everything and excludes nothing.

The third part of the ceremony, *expressing ways in which others have hurt us,* can progress only if the people in the group have the capacity to listen with calmness and attentiveness. When we have been hurt, Thây teaches, our "negative seeds" have been watered. The term "seeds" is a way of saying that the full range of our emotional life—seeds of delight, sorrow, disgust, courage, fury, desire, and so on—exist within us all. Events come along and water a seed or multiple seeds. The problem is not so much that we have, for example, a seed of anger—we all do. It's what we do with the energy of that anger once the seed has been watered that is important.

Before telling another of your distress, it's important that you have taken the time first to point out the other person's good qualities wholeheartedly. If you are angry or irritated with another to such an extent that you are unable to see his good qualities, you are not ready to speak. When you do speak, you can say, "My seed of _____ (fear, hurt, worry, anger) was watered when you said (or did) _____." The emphasis is less on what *the other* did and more on letting him know that *your* negative seed was watered. Once you've let him know, there is no need to embroider the story with details. You have let him know; he has received it in silence without defense or counterattack or explanation. If he needs to speak to you later, he can do so privately, calmly.

When all have had a chance to speak, the community shares some silence. The ceremony closes with the sharing of mindful breathing.

My own experience with this practice in groups is that the participants feel lighter within and warmer toward each other at the conclusion of the ceremony. Beginning Anew gives people a way to talk about what is working in their life together and what is not, and it offers possibilities for life-giving engagement and authenticity. This kind of attentiveness to negative feelings—and a ritual for its safe expression—does more for genuine community formation than all the appeals to charity and kindness can ever do.

Even if the group takes only a preliminary step toward appreciation and reconciliation, the dialogue has, in fact, begun. As Thây says, "Having begun anew, our life together can continue."

True Intimacy

After I returned home from my retreat with Thich Nhat Hanh, I suggested to my wife, Kathy, that Beginning Anew might be a good practice for us as a couple. We had been married for two years, a

second marriage for us both, and Kathy is indulgent of the ideas I
bring home to her in what she calls my role as our "advance spiritual scout." We regularly take a Sunday walk in the woods not far
from our home, and for us the walk seemed a natural time to incorporate this practice into our lives. We like the rhythm of walking
and talking, and knowing that Sunday is our day for Beginning
Anew gives us a reliable time to engage in the practice.

Here's how it works for us: One of us talks, and the other
listens without interrupting. We find it helps us listen well if we
follow the in and out of our breathing as we walk and listen. The
person speaking begins the first stage of Beginning Anew, appreciation, by saying, "What I've appreciated this last week has been
…" Simply knowing that we will be doing the practice each week
keeps us on the lookout during the week for what we appreciate.

It's interesting to be aware of what it's like to be appreciated
out loud. Kathy's appreciation sometimes stands in contrast to
the judgments of my inner "discrepancy monitor," by which I
measure myself against my ideals. Sometimes I notice myself
silently downplaying her appreciations, not really letting them
sink in. Simply noticing how I am closing myself off can have a
paradoxical effect: in the very act of noticing my closing, I begin
to open. Receiving Kathy's appreciation has something like the
tender effect of spring sun upon a blossom, and my body will
feel as if it is opening from its constrictions and armoring.

Sometimes I find myself hoping Kathy will notice aloud
something I want to be appreciated for. When I note this craving
for recognition, I can bring kindness to this craving. I'm now
practicing kindness, not craving. But, mostly, I am simply surprised and delighted by the things she notices, many that I
would never have appreciated in myself. Appreciation, I am
learning, is like psychological oxygen: we thrive in its presence
and begin to suffer in its absence.

The appreciation part of Beginning Anew is the fun part.
We then move on to the regrets part. While not necessarily fun,

voicing regrets can have the effect of opening the doors and windows and letting a fresh breeze inside the relationship. When I am talking about what I regret, I have a chance to notice aloud the gap between my intention and my execution. I can be clear about both the goodness of my intention, however imperfectly enacted, and what I've actually done or failed to do. For example, if I intend to be attentive, but, in fact, have been distracted, I can acknowledge this. I may have intended to be attentive (good in itself), but simply have failed to sustain my intention.

The practice invites me to notice what it is like to give voice to the regret. Is there some, or maybe a lot of, guilt? In voicing the regret, is there self-condemnation present? Is there remorse in the regret, an intention to change? Is there the hope that by confessing I will preempt the other's expression of hurt or anger?

The practice also invites me to notice what it is like to receive another's regrets. Am I holding on to a grievance after the regret is voiced, or am I letting go? I may find that I'm not ready to let go even though the other has acknowledged regret. How is the matter now for me? For the other? Has the air been cleared? Are there layers of an issue yet to be investigated?

Regrets are best voiced in a tone of nonjudgmental self-observation: "I noticed that I spoke with impatience, and I regret that." It is important that the person listening is doing just that: *listening*, not speaking. The one talking needs to be able to speak without interruption or comment. This simple ground rule is a key to the healing this practice brings. It is a great gift to have what you are saying received in such an unconditionally receptive way. While Kathy and I mostly confine our regrets to aspects of our own relationship, sometimes we may include regrets about another aspect of our lives. And there are many weeks during which no regrets arise and we can gladly announce, "Regrets, none." But there has never been a week in which there was nothing to appreciate about the other.

The hardest part of Beginning Anew is the last part, expressing ways in which your negative seeds have been watered. I have found it very helpful to have worked with at least some part of the RAIN protocol (see chapter 5) before I launch into the sharing of my negative seeds. Otherwise, Beginning Anew may serve as convenient cover for me to blast Kathy with blame. As Thich Nhat Hanh says in *Anger: Wisdom for Cooling the Flames*:

> When we suffer, we always blame the other person for having made us suffer. We do not realize that anger is, first of all, our business. We are primarily responsible for our anger, but we believe very naively that if we can say something or do something to punish the other person, we will suffer less. This kind of belief should be uprooted. Because whatever you do or say in a state of anger will only cause more damage in the relationship. Instead, we should try not to do anything or say anything when we are angry.

When one of my negative seeds has been watered, the first step of RAIN, recognizing, allows me to tell the truth to myself about what's happening. Emotions are like the weather: they blow in uninvited and, in time, any present emotion gives way to another weather system. Noting to myself "mind with irritation" or "mind with worry" lets me tell the truth to myself about what is undeniably the case—that irritation or worry is present even though I may not like it. Recognizing simply holds up a mirror, and says, "Yep, here's the desire to throttle this person."

In the presence of negative feelings, the second step of RAIN, accepting, invites me to stop fighting reality. I may not like the feeling of anger, for instance, but my resistance to the anger ("I shouldn't be feeling this or having to deal with this!") only adds to my suffering. The more I resist, the more the feeling persists. Sometimes I'll say to myself, "The sky is blue, the grass is green, and I'm furious." It's just a fact. If I'm having a recurrent emotion-laden thought, I can count its frequency over an hour or a day: judgment #403. I may wish to make a game of catching the thought or feeling by making a mark on a sheet of paper each time it arises.

It may not be until I say aloud to Kathy, "My seed of _____ (fear, hurt, worry, anger) was watered when you said (or did) _____," that I can move into the third step of RAIN, investigation. I can notice what it is like to say out loud that my negative seed of sadness, anger, or anxiety has been watered. I can check out if one kind of seed is easier to acknowledge to my partner than another. Do I have a shameful feeling about this negative seed of mine, namely that I shouldn't be having this envy or insecurity or competitiveness or indifference?

Or, if Kathy has told me about her negative seeds being watered, I can investigate what it is like to hear from her that I have watered her seed of impatience or anxiety. Do I inwardly tense in self-protection when she, even without blaming, tells me that I watered her seed of fear or anger? Can I notice my reactions and hold all of them in a gentle embrace? In other words, can I practice non-identifying with my own reactivity?

Zazen *in the Devil's Cauldron*

The thirteenth-century Japanese Zen teacher Dogen posed an arresting question: "Can you do *zazen* [sitting meditation] while sitting in the devil's cauldron?" In other words, can you be attentive and present to the moment when life is melting you down and everything in you wants to jump right out of this present moment?

Kathy and I had been incorporating Beginning Anew into our Sunday walks for about six months when she was diagnosed with breast cancer. Her diagnosis came on a Friday afternoon.

As we were weighing treatment options, Sunday came with our ritual of Beginning Anew. So we took to the woods and began our practice: "This is what I appreciate about you."

This phrase has a whole new power when you have been tossed into the devil's cauldron. Our weekly Beginning Anew practice had previously unfolded within the illusion of death-lessness. We had shared appreciation, regret, and negative seeds in the assumption that we had lots of time in front of us. Now we were newly aware of what Zen calls "the Great Matter of Life and Death." With the appearance of death as a new walking companion, a different poignancy entered our exchanges. Of course, death had been walking quietly with us all along; we simply hadn't noticed before. We also hadn't known before that this awareness of the possibility of death would bring a different dimension of love and understanding one another into our walks.

During the months of decision making, surgery, chemotherapy, and recovery, I don't know what we would have done without Beginning Anew. The practice gave us a dependable container to manage our feelings of fear as we sat in the devil's cauldron. Walking our way through the experience, we learned that each fearsome aspect of it, though unwelcome, was manageable, one step at a time. Within the structure of Beginning Anew, we found that we could talk about anything, especially those difficult things that we might have avoided out of fear of upsetting the other. With the usual structure of our lives upended, being able to give the gift of listening to the other, without the necessity of comment or solution, was priceless.

For an extended period of time around and after Kathy's surgery, the caring and worrying energy of friends and family moved in with us. The help from friends and family was invaluable, but it had a downside for me, over time. An introvert by nature, I was now beset with ever-present concern, a flood of casseroles, and nearly constant company, and I was not a happy camper with all these tent mates. Kathy and I couldn't have managed without the support, but I wanted our old life back, without all these helpers. I remember several months into the ordeal, after one particularly gruesome round of chemotherapy, we were walking and I was talking about my negative seeds. I said, "You know, I see why chemotherapy gets such a bad rap. I *hate* the suffering the chemo hits you with. This whole cancer deal has really watered my seed of aversion! And this is a little difficult to talk about, but as essential as this help has been, it's driving me crazy having all these people hovering around all the time. I liked our old life before all this."

Well, there it was, what I had a hard time saying, out there in the open. I remember the exact place in the woods, and how, once I had said it, the view seemed to open up. What had been constricted in me now was spacious, and we could both rail on and joke about the rottenness of this change that had come into our lives. We could speak to each other about what at times felt unspeakable, and begin anew. As one of my psychotherapy supervisors once observed to a group of us in training, understanding really helps.

Sometimes when we tell our stories and have them met with understanding, we are able to drop them. The limiting thoughts, beliefs, and judgments we have held about our situation give way to a larger understanding. A story of loss may drop away into a larger one of loss and gain.

Ram Dass tells one of my favorite stories in his memoir *Still Here.* The story is about a Chinese farmer who has a prized mare that ran away onto the vast surrounding steppes. His neighbors came to commiserate and talk about what a disaster this was. The farmer responded, "What makes you so sure this is a disaster?"

A week later his mare showed up again, trailing a big, beautiful stallion. The neighbors congratulated him on his good fortune. He replied, "What makes you so sure this is a blessing?"

Some time later, his son was riding the stallion, fell off, and was badly injured. Again the neighbors came to offer their condolences, and the farmer said to them, "What makes you so sure this is a disaster?"

Shortly thereafter, war came to this part of China and all the young men of the village were drafted into the emperor's service. Many subsequently perished, but the farmer and his son lived on to support each other.

Blessing and disaster follow one another, and who can rightly tell which is truly the blessing, and which truly the disaster?

Kathy and I knew we had come a long way in the cancer experience when we could acknowledge the blessings that had come in its wake, as well as the losses we would not have willingly chosen. We knew what Ram Dass calls "the paradox of misfortune." But whether the experience of the moment felt like a blessing or a disaster, the one dependable blessing we had was our weekly practice of Beginning Anew.

Buddhists like to talk about the Eight Vicissitudes: pleasure and pain, gain and loss, praise and blame, fame and disgrace. My teacher Phillip Moffitt calls these "the terrible twins." His point is that we don't get one of the twins without the other. We'd like to construct a life that is all pleasure, gain, praise, and fame. Who wouldn't? But our existence is inevitably marked by certain unsatisfactory realities, such as sickness, old age, and death, not to mention other lesser indignities. How we make our way through these realities, or better yet, how we use these realities to wake up, is the heart of spiritual practice.

A spiritual practice such as the regular ritual of Beginning Anew offers many blessings as we make our way through the vicissitudes life offers us: The blessing of noticing what is worthy of appreciation here and now, and naming these graces aloud. The blessing of clearing away the debris of regret, freeing us from the dead hand of the past for the life offered us here and now in the present moment. The blessing of telling the truth about the way things are for us, and having this truth carefully received.

The Sunday after I had heard my clients' "holiday horrors" story, Kathy and I made our way into the woods for Beginning Anew. A Christmas storm had coated the trees with prisms of ice through which the sun was now sparkling. All around was the snap, crackle, pop of the ice beginning to melt. The middle Tennessee hills had never looked so lovely, so spectacularly beautiful. Along our way, we would periodically stop our appreciations for one another to appreciate the scene before us in silence. It seemed the whole countryside was lit up with appreciation. It was good to be alive, and with each other.

Blessed Relief:
The Practice of Beginning Anew

Sometimes I wonder to myself why some people who know about a practice such as Beginning Anew choose not to undertake it. Certainly the electronic distractions available to all of us and the very obligations of family life can take their toll on the habits that nourish a life together. But more fundamental to the resistance to engaging in a regular practice like Beginning Anew is the very reason we so need it: the fear of being truly seen and known, and the fear of being truthful about what we see and know in the other.

At first this fear may express itself as awkwardness or unfamiliarity in self-disclosure. The rationalizations of "We love each other; we don't need to say it out loud" or "We like to be spontaneous rather than programmed" can contribute to reluctance to try this kind of exchange. Thich Nhat Hanh has been very helpful to me on this issue. He observes that unless there is understanding in a relationship, there is not love. And if there is little disclosure, there is little understanding. Have you ever had someone protest that they love you, yet all the while you are not feeling understood?

I now offer the practice of Beginning Anew to couples in premarital and marital counseling. Appreciation, or the watering of positive seeds, is a powerful practice in and of itself. It is vitally important for each of us to hear what is "not wrong" with us because many of us carry a deep wound inside that tells us there is, in fact, something very wrong with us. If two people set aside a protected time to make sure they intentionally water seeds of happiness in one another each week, they do themselves and each other a great service.

Beginning Anew can be done with another person or with a small group. If you are doing the practice with a group, each person who wishes to speak can move through all three pieces of appreciation, regret, and negative seeds before the next person begins. Alternatively, the whole group can do appreciation before moving on to regrets, and ending with negative seeds.

On any given day there may not be enough calmness to engage in the disclosure of regrets or how negative seeds have been watered. That's why beginning with appreciation is always desirable, even when you are burning with regret or a strong feeling about a wrong you feel you have suffered. Partners or groups may not be ready to go beyond appreciation until some level of trust has been built both in the safety of the process and in the carefulness of the other. Don't try to do this practice if you are in the middle of an emotional meltdown. Wait until you are in a calmer emotional space.

I like to practice Beginning Anew weekly, but it can be done at any time. I have found that the regular practice of Beginning Anew trains me in being able to give voice to appreciations, regrets, or negative seeds on the spot. The better you become at mindful speech in the moment, the richer the weekly ritual of Beginning Anew becomes. Give yourself the opportunity to practice this ritual with someone you care about.

- Begin with appreciation. Decide who will speak first, and who will listen. If you are the one speaking, say what you appreciate about the other person, what he or she has done or refrained from doing. Be specific. Talk about particular moments; give an example of what you are appreciating. If no appreciations come to mind, you may need to widen the lens of your awareness. The regular practice of Beginning Anew will help you be on the lookout for things to appreciate. The person listening does just that, silently receiving what is being said.

- The person speaking then moves to regrets. Regrets may be about things done or left undone, things said or left unsaid. Don't beat up on yourself about regrets. Just say, "I regret doing this." Avoid making excuses for why you did, or failed to do, something. Just say you regret it. Or, if you have no regrets at the moment, just say, "No regrets!" The person listening does not speak, absolve, accuse, or comment in any way. The one listening allows the regret to be articulated without comment. In this way, a receptive space is left around the words expressed and any feelings associated with them.

- Finally, the process moves to negative seeds, if any have been watered. These are usually seeds of fear and worry, anger and disappointment, sadness and despair. It is *very important* that these seeds be spoken of without blame or accusation, with the recognition that this is *the speaker's seed of negativity,* and that he or she is taking responsibility for taking good care of it. Speaking about the seed is for the purpose of disclosure and connection, not for revenge or retaliation. If you cannot speak about your negative seed without blame, it is best to remain silent until you can. Again, if there have been no negative seeds watered, you can say, "No negative seeds!"

- For the person listening to another's negative seed, the impulse to defend or attack or get away may arise. This is a moment when following your breath in and out can help a lot. Resist the impulse to speak; just listen. The other's telling about his or her negative seeds may water yours. If so, this is grist for the mill of mindfulness practice.

- After the person who is speaking has finished with appreciation, regret, and negative seeds, reverse roles so that the person who has been listening now becomes the speaker.

8

THE DHARMA OF DYING

Should someone ask
where Sokan went,
just say,
"He had some business
in the other world."

DEATH POEM OF YAMAZAKI
SOKAN, DIED CA. 1540

Remembrances

The night before my father's death, I had a dream of kayaking with some friends. We were getting into our kayaks when a much larger boat with a house perched on top came careening out of control down the channel before us. The pilot had lost control, and the boat struck a spit of land, flipped over on its side, then slowly turned all the way over so that the deck lay face down in the water, with the keel in the air. I said to my companions, "No one could have survived that." Just as we began paddling out to inspect the wreckage, I awoke from the dream.

Although none of the hospice nurses or doctors had yet concluded that my father's death was imminent, there was within me, on some level, a knowledge that my father's earthly end was at hand. In the morning following the dream, I found Dad comfortable but no longer conscious. As the day wore on, the sun slanting in through the blinds, I spent the late afternoon quietly holding his hand. My brothers and mother gathered around his bedside, saying goodbye, telling him it was okay to go. After my son, Alex, his only grandchild, had said farewell, my dad slipped away in the early evening.

The Buddha said that of all mindfulness practices, the meditation on death is supreme. Buddhist monks make a daily recitation of what is called "the Five Remembrances," a kind of Buddhist memento mori. The Five Remembrances invite us to see that our common lot in life is the reality of change: growing old, growing ill, dying, losing what is precious to us, and leaving behind the fruits of our actions. Dad had said to me a few months before his death, "This old body is just wearing out." He was growing old and knew he was ill and dying. He was preparing to let go of what had been precious to him. When he took leave of this life, he left behind the fruit of a lifetime of service.

A year before he died, my father told us a story we had never before heard. When he was twenty-five years old, Dad was a navy surgeon, operating on wounded marines from the First Marine Division in Korea. When he stepped off the boat in Korea, he immediately had five hundred wounded marines as patients, an overwhelming immersion in the suffering of illness and death. He saw many who would not live to grow old. During the first part of his military service, Dad operated on soldiers from the front lines in the navy's equivalent of a MASH unit. Later, he was sent to care for patients recovering at the naval hospital in Yokuska, Japan.

One day a patient in Yokuska heard my father's name paged and asked the nurse if he might speak to Dr. Peerman. This young soldier wanted to thank my father for saving his life back in Korea. Dad had operated on him after the boy's platoon had wandered into a minefield; he had amputated both of this boy's legs and an arm.

When Dad told this story, with seldom-shed tears, he wondered aloud if he really had done this boy any favor by saving his life. This soldier had lost so much that was precious to him. Even so, over fifty years after the encounter, Dad was still overwhelmed by the generosity of this soldier's thanks. Dad had enormous respect for the courage of those marines. He told me he wasn't afraid of death because he had seen so much of it when he was so young.

Once when he was operating aboard the USS *Consolation* during the war, a corpsman held up a telegram for him to read. It was the news that I had taken my first breath half a world away. After the war, Dad found himself drawn to obstetrics. Having seen so much suffering, he enjoyed delivering babies and being a part of so much happiness. It was a comforting symmetry that my father took his last breath in a hospital hospice unit that, years before, had served as a maternity ward where he had received many a newborn into this world.

Dad was a great lover of boats. Between my first breath and my father's last, there were many boats in our life together: canoes, kayaks, sailboats, and skiffs. I think he was happiest when he was on or near the water, and his idea of a great time was to board a freighter with my mother for a long passage somewhere. Dad could watch the crew at work, and he and my mother could dine with the captain and talk of sailors and ships and the sea. That evening of Dad's death, I marveled at the wisdom of the unconscious in choosing the imagery of a boat going down to tell me of his impending departure.

There was only one thing Dad wanted for his funeral—the navy hymn "Eternal Father Strong to Save." Dad had heard this hymn as he watched young soldiers and sailors being buried at sea, the refrain, "Oh hear us when we cry to thee for those in peril on the sea," accompanying them to their final rest in the deep.

At Dad's memorial service, it seemed fitting that we read from the Gospel of Mark the account of Jesus calming the wind and sea: "On that day, when evening had come, he said to them,

'Let us go across to the other side.' And leaving the crowd behind, they took him with them in the boat, just as he was" (4:35–41). My father, too, was making his passage to the other side, and he was taken, as are we all, "just as he was."

The Great Way

Jon Kabat-Zinn, founding director of the Stress Reduction Clinic at the University of Massachusetts Medical School, makes an observation in *Full Catastrophe Living* about weaving a parachute. He says that if you are going to jump out of a plane, it is wise to have begun weaving your parachute before you take the plunge. Fortunately, I had begun to weave the parachute of mindfulness practice some time before my father's dying, and like other contemplatives caring for the sick and dying, I found mindfulness practice made all the difference—especially as Dad descended into terminal agitation in his final weeks, when there was no more medical cure at hand. Practice helped me be present to whatever the moment was bringing, whether sweet or sad or maddening or humorous.

I found myself often moved to tears of gratitude for the great kindness of Willie Jackson, Dad's companion in the final weeks of his life. This giant of compassion was able single-handedly to move Dad physically from bed to chair and back again when the strength of Dad's legs had deserted him. Even more amazing to me, Willie was able to hold Dad emotionally, easing his suffering with a calming presence when no medicine seemed quite adequate to the moment. Willie and Dad had both been in the navy, and before Dad's terminal phase, they would talk about where the navy had taken each of them. When Dad would drift into a period of rest and quietness, Willie would reach into his backpack and draw out his book of Bible stories to read to himself. Willie told my father he would stay with him to the end, which is just what he did.

During the time of Dad's dying, Kathy reminded me of John Tarrant's remarkable account of his mother's death in *Bring Me the Rhinoceros*—remarkable in its lyrical and humorous honesty, and remarkable that this Zen teacher had just the word I needed to hear at the right moment, in this instance in the form of a Zen koan:

> *The great way is not difficult*
> *if you just don't pick and choose.*

As Tarrant's mother was dying, he noticed that whenever he found himself wanting anyone to be different, when he was picking and choosing for things to be other than they were, his mother's hospice room filled with sorrow and pain. But when he wanted no one to be different, when his own heart was spacious toward whatever was happening, the room was large and at peace.

Tarrant's simple observation was a lamp to guide me along the dying way with my father and my family. I, too, found that the way was not difficult if I wasn't picking and choosing. Not picking and choosing whether Dad was doing well or poorly. Not picking and choosing how we as a family were handling things. Not picking and choosing how others were reacting to this time in our family's life. Each moment, pleasant or unpleasant, was as it should be. Of course, there were moments when precisely what I was doing *was* picking and choosing. But noticing, "Ah, here's a moment of picking and choosing," offered me the freedom to choose. I could continue my struggling or I could drop picking and choosing in favor of being present in a more open and spacious fashion.

Along the way, there were decisions to be made about the particulars of Dad's care and the best setting for his care, decisions around the obituary and the memorial service, the burial and the family gatherings. In these decisions I found a focus and energy to do what needed to be done, but at night I found it hard to slow my mind and body down. I would awaken in the small hours, my mind slipping into the gear of what next needed to be done. When I became aware that this planning energy had taken over, I would purposely shift gears and listen to the night sounds, to the owls calling to each other in the autumn darkness. I would follow the tidal in-and-out of my breathing, letting the breath cradle and rock me back to sleep. To my surprise, I found myself enjoying the quiet and solitude of these nighttime awakenings—as long as I was not picking and choosing that I needed to be sleeping. Not picking and choosing, sleep would come again, all by itself, when it was ready. I couldn't help noting how easily my own breath came and how different it was from my father's labored breathing.

On the morning after my father died, I arose for my morning bike ride. The sun was just coming up, and on this first dawn without my father, I found myself pedaling in and through an unexpected beneficence. The soft pinks and salmon color in the sky, the familiar early bird sounds—these seemed to convey that all was well. A grouping of a dozen deer stood at attention as I rode past them—a quiet salute to my passing biking cortege.

Just a week before, I'd told Dad I'd seen a fox on my morning bike ride, an unusual sight, and he'd managed a slight smile. This morning he would not be there in the flesh to receive my story about what I had seen, so I found myself telling him right there, on the spot. And then, as I pedaled along, I wished my father well in Buddhist fashion, and to my surprise felt him wishing me well: "May you be filled with lovingkindness. May you be calm and peaceful. May you be safe. May you be well."

At the graveside service a few days later, I read the burial office from the Episcopal prayer book, and I offered my own remembrances for a small gathering of family and friends. My father's West Highland terrier, Bonnie, white ears pricked up, was seated next to my mother at the graveside. Alex read from Psalm 90:

"Lord, thou hast been our refuge from one generation to another."
After we had committed my father's ashes to the earth and to God,
Alex came and took the shovel from my hand, turning the first
spade of earth into the grave. As he reached for the shovel, Alex
touched me on the arm and whispered, "Good job, Dad."

Words of praise had never come easily from my father, and
I had spent much of my life longing for his approval. Hearing
these words from my son on the day of my father's burial was
mysteriously healing. The timing was perfect, the right word
from the right person at a moment with my heart wide open to
receive it.

I closed with the traditional Christian blessing: "The Lord
bless him and keep him, the Lord make his face to shine upon
him and be gracious unto him, the Lord lift up his countenance
upon him and give him peace." Then, in the Buddhist manner, I
wished my father well, and all of us gathered there well. The two
blessings gave voice to all I wished for my father and for all of us
in our family. This leave taking was a part of his life and of ours.
There was no resistance to the moment, no picking and choosing, no suffering. Just commending him and each other on the
great way. And gratitude for his life well lived.

Bowing to the Moment

Several weeks after Dad's death, I was scheduled to go on a
retreat for community dharma leaders at Spirit Rock Meditation
Center. I wondered whether to make this retreat, and if I did,
what would emerge emotionally. Unlike the usual silent retreat
format, I knew this gathering would be quite interactive in
nature, with a number of presenters and opportunities for small-
and large-group expression. I wasn't at all sure I was prepared
for immersion into such a lively group of ninety. Although I was
looking pretty normal on the outside, I wasn't feeling normal on
the inside.

Nonetheless, I decided to make the retreat, feeling there was something awaiting me. Once there, I often found myself mentally drifting back to the events of the past month and to memories of life with Dad and our family. Especially in the first few days, I was half in and half out of the retreat. Fortunately, with this group of people, I felt comfortable choosing when and to whom I wanted to reveal what was going on inside, but even so, it still felt a bit weird to be in the midst of so much activity so soon after Dad's death. I came to appreciate the wisdom of cultures that prescribe a period of mourning as a refuge from everyday demands following a death in the family.

From time to time, I would slip away from the group for a walk up into the mountains. On one walk, at the crest where the view stretches for miles all the way back to San Francisco Bay, I saw an enormous hawk circling, keening overhead. I found myself wishing the winged one well … and feeling the winged one blessing me back. Once again, just as on my morning bike ride, beneficence was here, all about me and within me. The best of Dad felt so present to me there, a blessing presence. All I had to do was step away from the busyness of the group into the refuge of the natural world to make contact.

At night I would hike up into the hills by the soft light of the moon. Up there, my father's passing at age eighty seemed part of the cycle of the seasons, part of an ancient, natural rhythm of taking birth and flourishing and taking leave. In the autumn's evening chill, as the moonlight lay across the land, the night sounds surrounded and comforted me, and a deep peace arose.

In this equanimity that attended me after Dad's dying, I seemed not to be having, in John Tarrant's phrase, "off the shelf" expectable feelings. I felt little sadness, more relief. I sometimes wondered, was there no grief within me at Dad's departure? It was in meeting with the *sangha* that an answer came to this question.

Jack Kornfield, one of the presenters on the retreat, offered us the practice of bowing as a way to be present to whatever the moment might bring, just as people in the East bow to one another with the greeting *namasté*. So it was bowing and *namasté* to the fog hanging on the hills in the morning, bowing to the steam rising from the oatmeal at breakfast, bowing to a moment of appreciation or joy or judgment or sadness or fear, bowing to the little fawn being licked by her mother. Whatever arose, bowing to it, holding it in loving awareness.

For me, bowing was especially helpful in the gaps between scheduled activities, such as walking to meals or in other non-structured time when the anxiety of self-consciousness would arise. On the usual silent retreat, the cocoon of silence would afford me the chance to hide out comfortably, but in this talking retreat structure there was far less continuous formal silent time and more triggers for social anxiety. Remembering to bow to my anxiety, especially since it was so familiar to me in group settings, was a whole new way to relate to my feeling.

When discomfort arose, either in interactions with others or in anticipation of them, I would inwardly bow to it. When I did, I found the bodily tension of the discomfort dropping into the space of awareness, and with this drop, liberating energies would move through my body. I was able to release long-held tension simply by being present to the discomfort in an open, flexible, and kind fashion. I became more comfortable with the discomforts of self-consciousness and almost began to look forward to moments when I could practice with them. Something was shifting within me, as well as between me and others.

The last presenter of the retreat was Joanna Macy, a wise woman, a teacher of engaged Buddhism and deep ecology. Joanna is a passionate presenter, herself open to the suffering of the human and what she calls the "more than human" world about us. She recalled for us the story T. H. White tells in *The Once and Future King*, of how Merlin taught the young Arthur the ways of the world by having him take on the form of various animals: falcon and ant and badger and goose. When the time came for him to pull the sword from the stone and take his rightful place as king, Arthur found he could not do it by ego strength alone. Only when he recalled his lives in the animal world and knew himself as belonging to this greater, more than human world, could he pull the sword from the stone, not for himself, but for the welfare of all beings.

Joanna then invited us to gather in groups of three and bring to mind a part of the world for which we had concern. It might be a place challenged by genocide, such as Darfur; a place such as Iraq where the violence of war and sectarian hatred reigned; a place confronting ecological disaster, such as the habitat of polar bears in the Arctic. First, we were to take on a human voice from that part of the world and for five minutes tell our partners what it was like to live in that place. My conversational partners took the voice of a woman refugee from Darfur and a young marine serving in Iraq. As each of us took on these voices, we found that they, in fact, took us over with an urgency and power we had not anticipated. All around the meditation hall we could hear people softly weeping at the stories being told.

After this first round, Joanna invited us to take on a more-than-human voice from the same place. It might be the voice of an animal, the voice of a feature of the natural landscape, such as a river, or the voice of a natural force, such as wind. One of my partners took on the voice of a little kitten from Baghdad, separated and lost from her family. This telling of the kitten's story deeply moved me and brought to mind my father's dog, Bonnie—how she lay by him as he struggled for breath in his last days, and how she must miss him now.

Somehow, in viewing my father's absence through more-than-human eyes, through Bonnie's eyes, the gates of grief, closed until that moment, opened. I found myself baptized in healing tears for Bonnie's loss, and for my own, for what had happened between my father and me, and for what no longer would. I felt anointed, blessed with tears of gratitude, tears of love. For several days I remained in this tender, open place.

I found myself wishing to name that this had occurred to the larger community dharma leader group, and when I did so, the group as one bowed in *namasté* to what I had shared. Privately, individually, with great sensitivity, people later spoke to me of what I had said and of what it was like for them to hear.

We all long for communities where we can show up and be ourselves and have our very self received without judgment. We long for communities where we can honestly name our struggle with what may be going on within the life of the community, not to find fault but as a matter of self-disclosure and authentic presence. We long for communities where we can be different and find, in and through and in spite of our differences, a belonging we scarcely have dreamed possible. Whenever we can bow without judgment to our own suffering and that of others, a blessed belonging takes place. When we know we truly belong, it is a blessed relief, worthy of a deep bow.

Old Wounds

A week after the retreat ended, I was back home, listening to a sermon in church. Our priest Becca Stevens was telling about an experience she'd had of being authentically herself in a large gathering of Christians, how she'd felt she belonged, in spite of all her differences with those present, just as she was. While listening to her, my mind flashed to a memory from college days, a memory of being in the operating room with my father.

During college summers, I had worked as an operating room technician and had often been able to watch my father perform surgery. I so enjoyed getting to know him there. I remembered the precision and care with which he would close the various layers of tissue in completing an operation, the clicking sound of the curved needle holders, the quiet competence with which he worked, the elegant closing of the skin at the end of the procedure. I remembered feeling proud of the way he cared for his patients and worked with the operating room staff. He was a gentle man.

With this image of my father closing a wound, I somehow intuited—in a way I cannot quite convey but surely knew—that an old wound was finally closing in me. Feeling not enough had been a wound that was a part of my relationship with my father. I longed for his blessing, a sense that I was, in his eyes, enough *just as I was.* There was in my dad, however, an improving, perfecting energy, and the blessing I longed for did not flow naturally from him. His daily example of dependability and honesty was itself a great gift to me, and I felt admiration for who he was and what he had done with his life. But he was a deeply private person, and we were not easily intimate with one another. Something in me felt outside his blessing.

In my own way, I tried to close the wound by various ego efforts, like the young Arthur, but no accomplishment was ever quite sufficient to bring about the blessing for which I longed. In fact, good work and recognition only added layer upon covering layer over the wound. The sometime-experience of failure and disappointment could easily rip through the covering layers to the underlying feeling not enough.

Remarkably, even though I knew the fix wouldn't work, the old strategy of trying to repair the wound with some good work would arise in me. I knew intellectually, of course, that no good work would ever bring the comfort in my own skin that I wanted, but this knowledge remained head knowledge, not deeply and inwardly known. I kept hoping somehow to win the blessing, if not from Dad then from any number of stand-ins. Disappointments in myself, leading to two periods of depression, left me with a sense of being beyond real and lasting repair.

Depression is a form of suffering that has been described as "the psychological crushing of bones," and this crushing has a particularly unremitting character. It was during the second depression that a friend threw me the life vest of mindfulness practice. When the undertow of depression almost took me down, mindfulness practice saved my life. Once I was back on firm ground, it gave me a way to enjoy this life.

A Zen master once said simply, "We are saved such as we are." Mindfulness has been such a blessed relief because it has given me a way to hold *everything* in my life compassionately, just as it is. Over years of practice, almost invisibly, mindfulness had been slowly stitching the old wound of feeling not enough. Sitting in church that day, I bowed to the wound in me, and I was able to receive my longing for Dad's blessing with kindness. Somehow I *knew* that the wound of feeling not enough was closing. In a quiet and confident way, I knew myself as enough, as one inside the embrace of love. I felt comfortable in my own skin.

After church I was walking in the park with Kathy, and along the way I found myself bowing to gain and loss, praise and blame, recognition and disgrace, pleasure and pain. I was not picking and choosing; all are part of my life, and all belong. Intimacy and non-intimacy belong. Belonging and not-belonging belong. Feeling enough and not enough belong. Even the wounds belong. And I belong, such as I am, to the community of those on the path to freedom, in the *sangha* and in the church.

As we can bow to the wounds in ourselves and the wounds in others, the wounds begin, in their own time, with grace, to close.

The great way is not difficult if we don't pick and choose.

Blessed Relief:
The Five Remembrances

The recitation of the Five Remembrances offers an embodied way to "teach us to count our days that we may gain a wise heart," as the psalmist puts it (90:12). The intention of this practice is to help you wake up to the significance of *this* moment, the impermanence of possessions and plans, and the significance of the actions you choose. Recited as a daily practice, the Five Remembrances bring relief to the suffering of loss by helping you hold these changes, without resistance, in mindful awareness. It is the dropping of resistance to these facts of life that brings relief from suffering.

Begin the practice by inviting your mind and body to be joined with awareness of your breath. After a few minutes of following the breath in silence, give voice to the Five Remembrances.*

> Breathing in, I know that I am of the nature to grow old.
>
> Breathing out, I know that I cannot escape growing old.
>
> *In-breath,* "Growing old" … *out-breath,* "No escape."
>
> (Repeat "Growing old … No escape" for a number of breaths)
>
> Breathing in, I know that I am of the nature to grow ill.
>
> Breathing out, I know that I cannot escape growing ill.
>
> *In-breath,* "Growing ill" … *out-breath,* "No escape."
>
> (Repeat "Growing ill … No escape" for a number of breaths)

Breathing in, I know that I am of the nature to die.

Breathing out, I know that I cannot escape dying.

In-breath, "Dying ... *out-breath,* "No escape."

(Repeat "Dying ... No escape" for a number of breaths)

Breathing in, I know that I will lose what is precious to me.

Breathing out, I know that there is no escape from losing what is precious to me.

In-breath, "Losing what is precious to me" ... *out-breath,* "No escape."

(Repeat "Losing what is precious ... No escape" for a number of breaths)

Breathing in, I know that the only thing I will leave behind is the results of my actions.

Breathing out, I know that there is no escape from leaving behind the results of my actions.

In-breath, "Results of my actions" ... *out-breath,* "No escape."

(Repeat "Results of my actions ... No escape" for a number of breaths)

* This is the form of the Five Remembrances practice given by Thich Nhat Hanh in *The Blooming of a Lotus.*

9

MOBILE LOAVES AND FISHES

For as long as space endures
And for as long as living beings remain,
Until then may I, too, abide
To dispel the misery of the world.

THE DALAI LAMA,
Nobel Peace Prize Lecture

Compassion Rising

"What is the climate of your heart?"

This is a question Sylvia Boorstein suggests we put to ourselves, kindly, from time to time. A psychotherapist, Buddhist meditation teacher, and observant Jew, Sylvia has been an inspiration to me since I first read her book *It's Easier Than You Think* when I was in a difficult time. On this particular retreat, however, I was not having a difficult time. Although the weather outside was unending rain, the climate of my heart was definitely happy.

The retreat had started out wonderfully. I had heard enthusiastic reports about a young Tibetan teacher named Tsoknyi Rinpoche, and when a spot opened up at the last minute for one of his retreats at Spirit Rock Meditation Center, I quite uncharacteristically dropped everything and flew to California. I don't know exactly what I was expecting when I first met him, but what I got was one of the funniest, lightest, happiest human beings I have ever encountered. When Tsoknyi walked into the meditation hall, it was as though the sun itself had come in to brighten the room. He was playful, mischievous, profound, and full of insight about American culture. America, he said, is very intelligent in terms of know-how, but things are "not so good" at the heart level, the level of know-why. He saw Americans as having "way too much on the hard drive. Need to press the delete button."

One of the great meditation masters of the twentieth century, Ajahn Chah, once said that 70 to 80 percent of the spiritual life is knowing you are grasping and not being able to do anything about it. If anyone was ever a walking advertisement for "nongrasping," it is Tsoknyi. He is open, carefree, happy, light. He knows how to use the delete button.

Grasping, says Tsoknyi, is like glue, what he calls "the full I/me glue" of our never-satisfied wanting. Picture a claw-like hand that is grasping, grasping, grasping, and you get a sense of what the everyday mind is like. Spiritual practice, in Tsoknyi's view, is letting go of grasping, and it begins with relaxing. As he writes in *Fearless Simplicity*:

> You have squeezed yourself so much—like a toothpaste tube. Everyone has squeezed themselves so much, you squeeze and squeeze until very little comes out. You have become completely dry, and no juice comes out, no juice at all. Relax, breathe in. Relax the feelings and sensations. This is necessary in order to relax, to be aware of how we are.

Relaxing and being "aware of how we are" is the prelude to recognizing the true nature of the mind, what Tibetans refer to as *rigpa*. *Rigpa* is self-existing awareness, essentially a space where the previous thought is gone and the future thought hasn't arrived yet, and a gap is evident. In the emptiness of this gap, we can discover our intrinsic nature. In *rigpa* the "I/me" thoughts, with all their glue and confusion, dissolve. When you recognize *rigpa*, there is a moment of full freedom: no glue, no grasping, just effortless awareness. This non-dual awareness is like an empty bowl, open to receive whatever the moment brings to fill it. The contents of the bowl may change from moment to moment, but awareness itself remains endlessly receptive, rejecting nothing.

Tsoknyi's teaching and presence were inspiring to me, but in the meditation sessions I was having no luck doing what we had come for, recognizing *rigpa*. Enough experience has taught me that stillness and stir-up in the mind on retreat are like yin and yang, one giving birth to the other, but I just wasn't getting it. Instead of effortless awareness, I was trying to "get" *rigpa*, thus ensuring, of course, that I would not. All I got was a lot of glue. Grasping, not being able to do much about it.

My doubts notwithstanding, almost a week into the retreat, during the first sitting one morning, *rigpa* came. Before the sitting, I had said to myself, "Just soften, just relax." As Tsoknyi had taught us, I followed my breath for a while (*shamatha*), then sat in choiceless awareness (*vipassana*), and then opened my eyes to rest in effortless awareness. When I finally relaxed and sat loosely, a profound stillness came. The "I" dropped away as unnecessary baggage, and an open awareness arose, not just "out front" in the visual field, but more in a 360-degree way. There were no pealing bells, no fireworks, nothing special ... but internally it felt as if the lights had come on.

At the end of the sitting, quiet tears of gratitude, for my family and teachers and friends, streamed down my face. I felt a deep, deep release. Blessed relief. I looked up toward the altar in the front of the meditation hall where a photograph of the Dalai Lama smiled back at me, full of benevolence and lightness. It was Good Friday morning. I found devotion arising toward

Jesus and Mary as I had never felt before. I laughed at Christian devotion arising in the Buddhist meditation hall. *Emma Ho.* How amazing!

As I was walking down the hill to breakfast, the sun was coming up, newly lovely after relentless rain during the week. The empty, open awareness of the sitting continued, and at breakfast my heart was open, just noticing without judgment. A woman in purple who had silently gotten under my skin all week came into view, and compassion toward her arose, naturally, without trying.

There are multiple layers to the experience of *rigpa*, but perhaps one of the most intriguing is that, in *rigpa*, we are in a kind of emptiness, but we are also feeling something more vast. As Tsoknyi describes it, "Within this openness, compassion just unfolds ... a deep-felt sense of being tender ... and somewhat delighted at the same time. There's a mixture; that is the true compassion."

Back home in the meditation group that Kathy and I lead, we end our sitting in Buddhist fashion with what's called a dedication of merit, a reminder of why we practice. "May the merit of our practice be for the welfare of all beings, and for the ending of suffering." These words remind us that our practice is not for ourselves alone, but for the welfare of all beings. The fruit of meditation is compassionate action, and this compassionate action is not first something we *do,* but who we *are.* The active doing arises out of the being.

In *rigpa*, we get a taste of who we are, recognizing our natural state of compassion, "tender and somewhat delighted." As Tsoknyi puts it, "We need to *be* compassion, to be in such a way that our identity is compassion itself." When we recognize our true nature and *are* compassion, everything we meet will be marked by our compassion—much as if we had turned into charcoal, as Tsoknyi describes it, and would mark whatever we would rub against, naturally.

Beyond Us and Them

In my classes on Buddhist-Christian dialogue at Vanderbilt Divinity School, it is not uncommon for students of Christian theology to ask, "Doesn't all this meditation lead to passivity or resignation or indifference in the face of suffering and injustice? What about fixing what's wrong in the world rather than all this talk about surrendering?" These students rightly wonder if something important isn't being left out with the move toward inward meditation.

I sometimes respond to them with a story that Guy Armstrong, one of the Spirit Rock teachers, tells about a Zen master who was asked, "Why is it that we spend all this time in meditation? What's the point of it all?" Guy was expecting to hear a famously dramatic Zen answer but, instead, the Zen master said simply, "An appropriate response."

The capacity to give an appropriate *response,* not a reaction, comes from moment-to-moment mindful practice with our own suffering. *Reactions* to suffering and injustice arise naturally, but these are often reactions arising from aversion and judgment, reactions that split the world into good and evil, us and them, the right and the wrong, the just and the unjust. Unfortunately, actions arising from aversive reaction often feed the very thing they oppose: the hatred of one camp sparking and justifying the hatred of the other.

In a dharma talk, "Seeing Suffering Directly," Jack Kornfield notes the ways we separate the world into categories of us and them. Whenever we have a sense of us—whether it's a matter of race or nation or age or religion—we have created a sense of "other."

> We really have to look at how we make separation.... Who is your "us"? On this planet at this moment, we are all of us together. We must touch that in ourselves. I don't care how you touch it. You can sit in *zazen* meditation or

you can march in New York. But if you haven't understood that, then it's still going to be "us" marching and
"them" outside or "us" sitting and "those" not sitting. Do
whatever it takes to touch that. See where your "us" is
and where your boundaries are. See that they don't work,
that any "us" and "them" is not going to be the source of
world peace and joy.

These words spoke to my heart when first I heard them because
I have seen this habitual, instinctive energy to split the world into
camps of us and them, my people and their people, within
myself. I have seen it in the Christian culture wars, whether the
splitting comes from the religious right or from the religious left.
I have seen how little good comes from mutual demonizing; it's
more often the reptilian brain fight/flight reaction than wise
response. I have seen how well-intended activism without contemplative compassion tends to polarize the world into victims
and victimizers. I have seen how splitting leads to more suffering.

For years, I have been learning from Buddhists how to
meditate, how to calm the mind and open the heart in the face
of the instinctive reaction to make someone else "them." In a
way I did not anticipate, it was this training in Buddhist mindfulness meditation that laid the groundwork for Christians to
teach me how to truly activate.

As my friend and colleague John Thatamanil, with whom
I co-teach the Buddhist-Christian dialogue class, observes,
"Buddhists are teaching Christians to meditate, and Christians
are teaching Buddhists to activate." For some time, I had been
on the lookout for my own genuine point of engagement between
contemplative practice and social justice. The Christians were
about to teach this meditator to activate.

It's said that when the student is ready, the teacher appears.
The teacher this time was a Texan, and he invited me to join him
on a retreat in Austin unlike any I'd undertaken before.

A Retreat on the Streets

On January 3, 2007, I was driving around minding my own business, when a story came on National Public Radio (NPR) about an organization in Austin, Texas, called Mobile Loaves and Fishes. It started in 1998 when several friends from a Catholic parish were talking about a ministry in Corpus Christi that provided blankets and hot drinks to homeless people on cold nights. One of the friends in Austin had a thought: what if we took food out to the homeless, where they lived, on the streets, in parks, under bridges, instead of requiring that they come to central dispensing soup kitchens and shelters?

This thought has grown into a social outreach ministry to the homeless and the working poor in Austin and beyond. Alan Graham, a real estate developer who first had the thought, shared it with some friends, who then loaded up a van with seventy-five sack lunches and hit the streets, guided by another friend who had been homeless since his childhood. Three months later, they had raised enough money to purchase a truck outfitted with a catering bed to feed the homeless and working poor.

Today, Mobile Loaves and Fishes (MLF) has over nine thousand volunteers from over seventy churches, schools, businesses, scout troops, and other organizations who served a quarter of a million meals to the homeless and working poor in six different cities last year alone. Listening to that NPR story, I thought, "It would great to have Mobile Loaves and Fishes in Nashville," so I looked up MLF on the Internet. Impressed by what I saw, my next thought was, "It would be good to call up Alan Graham and see about this."

Not in all my years have I ever had the thought that it would be good to call up someone after hearing an inspiring story on NPR—and I've heard many. But this thought continued to resonate within me, and quite uncharacteristically, I made the call.

That one call launched a chain of events that was about to change my life. It wasn't long before I was on a plane with my brother, Bill, and our longtime friend, Rob Barrick, to visit the mother ship of Mobile Loaves and Fishes at St. John Neumann Catholic Church in Austin. On our first truck run, we went to parks, alleys, parking lots, a halfway house for men just out of jail, and weekly-rate motels that charge the homeless and working poor $200 per week for "housing." When the truck pulled up, Alan honked the horn, and people came out of the darkness—old people, young people, children. They were so grateful for our showing up. When I saw boys the age of my own son, their faces full of sweetness and vulnerability, my heart just broke open.

We asked what they wanted to eat, to give them some choice, some dignity in having a choice. We shook hands, made contact, and conversations began. I noticed one man with a beautiful walking cane, and I said, "Man, I really like your cane. Where'd you get it?"

"I made it myself," he said.

"How'd you do these drawings on the carvings?"

"Oh, you know, with … what do you call them … colored pencils."

I said, "Oh, okay. That's really beautiful."

He smiled broadly.

With that exchange, "the homeless" stopped being a category, a *them*. "The homeless" became a man with a cane he'd made himself. I saw a woman with a crack habit, whom Alan offered to get into a treatment program. I saw a man selling "Free Hugs" buttons. A man crying and asking if we had seen his friend. Another man who came running back to the truck, saying, "I was so happy eating my meal I forgot about my girlfriend. I was supposed to get one for her. I stopped eating my food and came back for her. Now that's true love." We all had a big laugh.

After giving out all the food, the truck team went out to dinner together. Bruce Agness, Alan's longtime sidekick and MLF

founding member, who had made the truck run with us, listened
to all our questions at dinner. Then he looked us in the eye and
said, "Don't worry too much about how all of this is going to
come together. Just go ahead and do it."

And so we did. Mobile Loaves and Fishes has come to
Nashville. We made our first truck run a mere six months after I
heard the NPR story.

Softening the Heart

"In Tibet there is a lot of livestock." With this simple statement,
Tsokyni offers a humble illustration that is eye-opening—heart-
opening, really. Though we don't have a lot of yaks running
around the country, surely we can understand the analogy he
lays out in *Fearless Simplicity*:

> The skin from these animals needs to be cured in order
> to be useful: it needs to be softened by a special process.
> Once hide is cured, it becomes flexible and can be used
> in all sorts of ways.... But first it needs to be prepared in
> the right way: it needs to be softened, made flexible. If
> the hide is simply left as it is, it hardens and becomes
> totally stiff; then it is nothing but an unyielding piece of
> animal skin. It is the same ways with a human being's
> attitude. We must soften our hearts, and this takes delib-
> erate effort.

This softening of the heart is the spiritual path, and it's an ongoing, ever-deepening inside job. Our work, our inner work, is to
transform anger into justice, hurt into compassion, suffering
into wisdom.

Each time we take a Mobile Loaves and Fishes truck out,
we pray, "God of the poor and afflicted, soften the hard edges of
my heart that I might see your image in the eyes of those who

are outcasts in our world. Open me to embrace those who are hungry and abandoned. Soften me to understand the angry and the desperate. Enliven me to offer my gifts and treasures to the stranger and alien. Empower me with compassion toward the imprisoned and forgotten. Enflesh my heart with the loving heart of Jesus, who lived among us to point the way to your reign of justice and dignity."

On one of our first runs in Nashville, we came across a man resting against a bridge railing on a mercilessly hot, late summer afternoon. We stopped the truck and asked if he was hungry.

Seeing the Mobile Loaves and Fishes logo on the truck, he asked almost unbelievingly, "Y'all got food?"

We said, "You bet, we got food."

As he received his dinner, he said with a big smile, "Hebrews 13:2." He waited for us to quote chapter and verse, and not hearing an immediate recitation from us, he kindly offered, "Be not forgetful to entertain strangers, for thereby some have entertained angels unawares" (KJV).

Waving us goodbye, this man with no home had blessed us on our way. We looked at each other and shook our heads, tears in our eyes.

In one of his best-known teachings, Jesus said in the Sermon on the Mount:

> Blessed are you who are poor,
> for yours is the kingdom of God.
>
> Blessed are you who are hungry now,
> for you will be filled. (Luke 6:20–21)

Again and again with Mobile Loaves and Fishes, we have found ourselves at the door of the kingdom in the presence of the poor. We have found ourselves filled to overflowing by their gratitude, our hearts softened by their generosity of spirit. I am reminded of the Tibetan word for "compassion," *nyingje*. *Nying* means "heart" and *je* means "the most eminent." I like the way they come together to suggest that what takes the most eminent seat in the heart is compassion.

I've learned a lot about compassion from both Christian and Buddhist teachings. Both activating *and* meditating soften the heart, and each needs the balancing effect of the other. In Christian language, the two sisters Mary and Martha need one another; the contemplative life (Mary) needs the active life (Martha). Without the active life, the contemplative life may turn its gaze away from suffering and injustice, neglecting what Jews call *tikkun olam*, the call to heal, transform, and repair the world. Without the contemplative life, the active life can burn itself out, like a forest fire eventually consuming the very fuel on which it spreads.

I remember when a Catholic priest who had powerfully inspired me in my own priestly vocation became so depleted in his active ministry that his body threw one illness challenge after another at him. But he refused to slow down because there was work, good work, to be done, and he kept pushing through his exhaustion. After his inevitable collapse, he dreamed that he was trapped in an attic so completely cluttered with furniture that he could find no way out. He later told me on his hospital bed that he hadn't taken time for solitary prayer in years.

One Buddhist teacher tells of feeling powerful energetic currents coursing through her body after deeply concentrated meditations, sensations at first blissful but, over time, more disturbing than delightful. After a period of growing distress at these uncomfortable energies, she consulted a respected Tibetan teacher, who asked her, "How much Compassion practice are you doing?" As she opened her heart to the suffering of others through Compassion meditation, the energies moderated and leveled out.

This need for balancing action and contemplation comes home for me in the words of Father Thomas Keating, who teaches that there are two great gifts of God: *just to be* and *just to do*. We can't *just do* until we have learned to *just be,* and it is out of the experience of *just being* that we can find contentment in the joy of *just doing*. As Keating writes in *The Heart of the World,* "We need to return to these two great capacities again and again and cultivate them."

There is not one of us who is *not* touched by suffering. In the face of inequalities and social miseries, there is not one of us who has *not* been angered by injustice, whether inflicted on us personally or directed at someone called "them." There is not one of us who has *not* been hurt by unkindness ... and there is not one of us who has *not* acted both unjustly and unkindly. Anger and hurt harden the heart, whether we're on the giving or receiving end. Learning how to *just be* with the suffering of anger and hurt in meditation softens the heart. Resting in spacious awareness, we become compassion for ourselves and for all beings. The point of meditation is to see clearly our own grasping and aversion and clinging, as well as that of others, and to name it: this is suffering. Only then can our response to suffering arise out of true compassion.

When compassion arises naturally, we learn how to *just do* what needs to be done in the face of suffering, and in the doing our hearts are further softened. When I am being and doing with the homeless and working poor, my heart is softened by the way they say thank you. They say, "God bless you." Never before have I felt so well blessed as by their blessings.

It is no wonder that Keating says we need to cultivate the balance: There is not one of us who does *not* need both to *just be* and to *just do*. In conversations between Buddhists and Christians, a bridge between action and contemplation is being laid down. Buddhists are teaching Christians to just be, and Christians are teaching Buddhists to just do. Engaged Buddhists, such as Thich Nhat Hanh, Roshi Bernie Glassman, Gary Snyder, and Robert Aitken Roshi, are working with prisoners, working to care for the environment, working to care for the dying, working to teach nonviolence and peacemaking. Contemplative Christians, following the lead of Thomas Merton and Thomas Keating, Dom Bede Griffiths and Father John Main, Brother Wayne Teasdale and Brother David Steindl-Rast are teaching people how to meditate within the Christian tradition. On the bridge of compassion, the traffic flows both ways: Buddhists and Christians learning from one another how to meditate and how to activate, how to soften the heart.

Blessed Relief:
Compassion Practice

Invite the mind and body to settle as you sit. Listen to the ambient sounds around you, allowing each sound to be just as it is. After a few minutes, focus your awareness on the sensations in your body, allowing these sensations to arise and pass away just as they are. Then, in your own time, notice how your body is receiving and releasing your breath, how the body is a swinging door with outside air coming in and inside breath going out. Allow the breath to be just the way it is.

Now bring to your mind someone for whom you deeply care, someone who is suffering either emotionally or physically. Picture this person in all her or his uniqueness and goodness. As your heart softens, make a heart-to-heart connection, saying silently, "May you be free from suffering. May you be happy." Then imagine it so. Imagine that your heartfelt prayer for this person has come to pass. Feel in your body what this compassionate intention is like.

Now bring to mind someone who has helped you on your life journey who you know is suffering. Just as you did before, when you sense a heart-to-heart connection, wish that this person might be free from suffering and happy. You may like to say on the in-breath, "May you be free from suffering," and on the out-breath, "May you be happy." Repeat this prayer for as long as you like, joining the breath of life to your compassionate wish.

Then think of a person or group of people whom you do not personally know but who is suffering. Again, picture this person vividly in your mind's eye. As your heart softens to him or her, offer your prayer, repeating the phrases that give voice to your compassionate intention. You may use phrases other than those suggested here; any words that express the goodwill of your heart are good.

The next step is challenging. Bring to mind a person or a group of people who has hurt you or someone else. Know that whatever her or his actions, this person has acted out of ignorance: fear, aversion, and non-understanding. As you bring this person to mind, see if your heart is willing to wish that she or he might be free from suffering and be happy, even though this person has caused suffering. If your own heart is hardened, do not judge yourself in any way, but see this as your own suffering and offer the wishes of freedom from suffering and happiness to yourself.

Whatever your own suffering, picture yourself in a way that your heart softens to yourself. Some people find that picturing themselves as a child or infant helps. "May I be free from suffering. May I be happy." Imagine it so.

Finally, cast the widest possible net with your compassion, wishing that all beings everywhere might be free from suffering, that the whole planet might be happy. And imagine it so.

Afterword

In *One Dharma: The Emerging Western Buddhism*, Joseph Goldstein distinguishes two basic styles of practice that lead to freedom from suffering: building from below and swooping from above.

Building from below begins with noticing the suffering that attends the grasping and clinging mind. Investigating this suffering, we will inevitably find stories about how we believe things should or shouldn't be. When we build from below, we practice letting go of these stories and our attachments to the way we want things to be.

Swooping from above, on the other hand, begins with a glimpse of "the open, innate wakefulness of mind." This is a seeing into awareness itself as the space within which thoughts and feelings arise apart from any particular content of the mind. Swooping from above invites a seeing into the essence and true nature of the mind when it is open and free of grasping and clinging.

We need to discover, Goldstein teaches, which approach might be more useful at a particular moment. Building from below is more likely to help us when we are lost in endless analysis and endless emoting, when our minds are distracted and restless. It's hard to rest in awareness when we're caught in the clutches of suffering. On the other hand, when we are striving very hard to be free of suffering through our building from below practices, it can be liberating to swoop in from above and see that what we are looking for, the open, innate wakefulness of mind, is already here. This recognition "could be just what is needed to relax the mind into a place of greater ease and freedom.... And even if it is only a glimpse of 'sudden awakening,' it can transform how we understand the difficulties that still arise."

In the retreat experiences that link the chapters of this book, I have built from below and swooped from above. Both approaches have led me on a pathway of stillness, silence, and moments of awakening. Since beginning to walk this Buddhist path, I have wanted to bring some of the practices so freely offered to me by Buddhists to people walking the Christian way. For the last decade in my work as a therapist and teacher of mindfulness-based stress reduction, I have seen how both building and swooping bring relief to people who would not necessarily have thought to seek relief in the teachings of the Buddha. They weren't looking for Buddhism, but for an end to their suffering. This is what the Buddha taught, an end to suffering and the possibility of freedom.

Not long ago Kathy and I offered a weekend of mindfulness practice at St. Mary's Sewanee, an Episcopal retreat center on the Cumberland Plateau in Sewanee, Tennessee. We titled the retreat "Mindfulness: The Master Skill for Happiness." The retreat was an invitation for all of us to move from expectation to possibility, from the rigidity of how we believe things "ought" to be into an openness to meet things just as they are. Our basic tool for the retreat was relaxed, embodied awareness, Phillip Moffitt's definition of mindfulness. We practiced awareness of breathing, awareness of the soundscape and the landscape, awareness of walking and sitting and moving and eating. We noted the ever-changing contents of the mind stream, how the mind has preferences of "for" and "against" the way things are. We practiced inclining the mind to happiness, looking for the good, and choosing to take actions that would lead to happiness.

Almost all of those who came for the retreat were Christians or had been raised in Christian churches. Some had suffered large, recent losses. Many said they weren't quite sure what they were getting into by coming to the retreat. But by the end of the weekend, many found that they had tasted for themselves the freedom that comes from mindfulness practice. In the silence and stillness of the mountains, we tasted what the Buddha called the "One Taste" of all spiritual paths, the taste of freedom. We knew moments of release from grasping and clinging and glimpsed what Buddhists call "crossing over" to the other shore of freedom. Beyond expectation, we found that moments of happiness were possible, no matter what our suffering.

On the last morning of the retreat, we did qigong while looking out across the valley, where morning clouds were nestled into the hollows of the land below. In the early morning stillness, as we did a movement called "Opening the Heart on Top of the Mountain," the words of an ancient Christian refrain came to mind: *sursum corda*, lift up your hearts. When the mind is calm, the heart naturally lifts.

We sat in silence in front of an exquisite icon of the risen Christ, his hand raised in blessing. In effortless attentiveness we noticed sounds and bodily sensations, thoughts and feelings, all arising and passing away. Allowing things to be as they were, we turned to look into the stillness and gently inquired into who or what was aware. We found there wasn't any "one" there, but awareness itself, shining through the eyes of each one of us. What we all were looking for was what was looking through us, and through all of creation.

In the stillness after the morning sitting, bowing in gratitude, I could hear the voices of my Buddhist teachers:

> *Receive the in-breath. Release the out-breath.*
> *Relax and sit loosely.*
> *Just this breath. Just this step. Just this.*

It's already here.
Allow everything to be as it is.
Look. See. Let go. Be free.

Mindfulness practice gives us a way to allow things to be as they are, for this present moment cannot be different than it is. Out of the equanimity that comes from letting things be as they are, we then can compassionately choose what action to take in the face of suffering. This equanimity, together with naturally arising compassion, transforms suffering into freedom. Whenever we can hold our stories of how things ought to be in kind, spacious awareness, the grip of suffering loosens, and with blessed relief, we find freedom. I like the saying of the Indian sage Ramakrishna: "The winds of grace are always blowing, but we have to raise our sails to catch them."

Mindfulness practice is one way to catch the winds of grace.

Glossary

accedia Sadness, spiritual torpor, sloth. A term used by Christian monks to describe a state of restlessness and inability to work or pray.

ascesis Exercise, training. A term used by Christian monks to describe a system of practice to combat vice and develop virtue.

big mind Buddhist formulation for the mind that is open to all that is; the mind that does not split experience into dual pairs of opposites such as good/bad or right/wrong, but sees beyond conventional dualistic thinking.

bodhi Pali word for the light within, enlightenment, or awakening.

chochma Hebrew word for wisdom.

dedication of merit Words recited at the end of sitting meditation, for the end of suffering and the welfare of all beings.

dharma Sanskrit word for the Buddha's teaching; the "way" or "truth" or "law"; "the way things are" or "how things stand."

dukkha Pali word for suffering, unsatisfactoriness.

Eight Vicissitudes A Buddhist list of eight mental factors: pleasure/pain, praise/blame, gain/loss, recognition/disgrace.

Emma Ho Tibetan phrase meaning "How amazing!"

Five Hindrances A Buddhist list of five impediments to clear seeing: grasping, aversion, restlessness, fatigue, doubt.

Five Remembrances A Buddhist meditation on old age, sickness, death, the impermanence of one's possessions and relationships, and the ongoing fruits of one's actions.

Four Noble Truths The most basic teaching of the Buddha: there is suffering, suffering comes from grasping, there is an end to suffering, there is a way to end suffering.

gate, gate, paragate, parasamgate, bodhi svaha Sanskrit words concluding the Heart Sutra, translated as "Gone, gone, gone all the way from suffering to liberation, everyone gone, praise to awakening!" The refrain is an expression of the movement from suffering to liberation, from forgetfulness to mindfulness, from duality into non-duality.

mindfulness A quality of mind that notices what is happening in the present moment with no clinging, aversion, or delusion. The Pali word for mindfulness is *sati*. Mindfulness is said by Thich Nhat Hanh to be "the heart of the Buddha's teaching."

metta Pali word for lovingkindness.

namasté Sanskrit word that literally means "I bow to you."

nirvana Sanskrit word for cessation of suffering; the liberation from all greed, hatred, and delusion in the mind of an enlightened being.

nyingje Tibetan word for compassion.

rigpa Tibetan word for the true nature of the mind; non-dual awareness.

samadhi Sanskrit word for concentration.

samsara Sanskrit word for the endless cycle of birth and death.

sangha Pali word for the entire community of beings; the Buddhist community.

sawu bona Common greeting among the tribes of northern Natal in South Africa, meaning "I see you"; the response is *sikkhona*, "I am here."

shamatha Sanskrit word for calm abiding; following one's breath.

small mind Buddhist formulation for the narrow, grasping mind, reaching out whenever it can for pleasure, praise, recognition, or gain; the dualistic mind that splits experience into opposites.

tanha Pali word for thirst, grasping, longing, craving, desire.

thin place Celtic Christian term for a place where the Presence is so strong it feels like a portal between worlds.

tikkun olam Hebrew; Judaism's call to heal, transform, and repair the world.

vipassana Pali word for insight; insight meditation; seeing clearly; meditation that focuses on the basic nature of the mind body process to understand its true characteristics.

zazen Japanese word for sitting meditation.

Suggested Resources

Books

Adyashanti. *Emptiness Dancing*. Boulder, CO: Sounds True, 2006.

Bamberger, John Eudes, trans. *Evagrius Ponticus: The Praktikos & Chapters On Prayer*. Spencer, MA: Cistercian Publications, 1980.

Bayda, Ezra. *Being Zen: Bringing Mediation to Life*. Boston: Shambhala Publications, 2002.

Bennett-Goleman, Tara. *Emotional Alchemy: How the Mind Can Heal the Heart*. New York: Harmony Books, 2001.

Boorstein, Sylvia. *Happiness Is an Inside Job: Practicing for a Joyful Life*. New York: Ballantine Books, 2008.

————. *It's Easier Than You Think: The Buddhist Way to Happiness*. San Francisco: HarperCollins, 1997.

Brach, Tara. *Radical Acceptance: Embracing Your Life with the Heart of a Buddha*. New York: Bantam Books, 2003.

Chödrön, Pema. *Start Where You Are: A Guide to Compassionate Living*. Boston: Shambhala Publications, 2003.

————. *When Things Fall Apart: Heart Advice for Difficult Times*. Boston: Shambhala Publications, 2005.

Dass, Ram. *Still Here: Embracing Aging, Changing, and Dying*. New York: Riverhead Books, 2001.

Dunne, John S. *The Way of All the Earth: Experiments in Truth and Religion*. Notre Dame, IN: University of Notre Dame Press, 1978.

Frazier, Jan. *When Fear Falls Away: The Story of a Sudden Awakening*. San Francisco: WeiserBooks, 2007.

Gimian, Carolyn Rose. "The Three Lords of Materialism." In *The Best Buddhist Writing 2006* by Mcleod, Melvin ed. (Boston: Shambhala Publications, 2006), 149–159.

Goffman, Erving. *The Presentation of Self in Everyday Life*. New York: Peter Smith Publisher, 1999.

Goldstein, Joseph. *One Dharma: The Emerging Western Buddhism*. New York: HarperCollins, 2003.

Hanh, Thich Nhat. *Anger: Wisdom for Cooling the Flames*. New York: Riverhead Books, 2001.

———. *The Blooming of a Lotus: Guided Meditation for Achieving the Miracle of Mindfulness*. New York: Beacon Press, 1999.

———. *The Heart of Understanding: Commentaries on the Prajnaparamita Heart Sutra*. Berkeley: Parallax Press, 1988.

———. *The Long Road Turns to Joy: A Guide to Walking Meditation*. Berkeley, CA: Parallax Press, 1996.

———. *The Path of Emancipation*. Berkeley, CA: Parallax Press, 2000.

———. *Peace Is Every Step: The Path of Mindfulness in Everyday Life*. New York: Bantam Books, 1992.

———. *Touching Peace: Practicing the Art of Mindful Living*. Berkeley, CA: Parallax Press, 1992.

Huber, Cheri. *Be the Person You Want to Find: Relationship and Self-Discovery*. Murphys, CA: Keep It Simple Books, 1997.

Jenkins, Sara ed. *Sweet Zen: Dharma Talks from Cheri Huber*. Murphys, CA: Keep It Simple Books, 2000.

Johnston, William, ed. *The Cloud of Unknowing and The Book of Privy Counseling*. New York: Image Books, 1973.

Kabat-Zinn, Jon. *Full Catastrophe Living: Using the Wisdom of Your Body and Mind to Face Stress, Pain, and Illness*. New York: Dell Publishing, 1990.

———.*Wherever You Go, There You Are: Mindfulness Meditation in Everyday Life*. New York: Hyperion, 2005.

Katie, Byron. *Loving What Is: Four Questions That Can Change Your Life*. New York: Three Rivers Press, 2003.

Keating, Thomas. *The Heart of the World: A Spiritual Catechism*. New York: Crossroad, 1989.

———. *Invitation to Love: The Way of Christian Contemplation*. New York: The Continuum International Publishing Group, 2006.

———. *Open Mind Open Heart: The Contemplative Dimension of the Gospel*. New York: Continuum International Publishing Group, 1994.

Kornfield, Jack. *After the Ecstasy, the Laundry: How the Heart Grows Wise on the Spiritual Path.* New York: Bantam Books, 2001.

————— *A Path with Heart: A Guide through the Perils and Promises of Spiritual Life.* New York: Bantam Books, 1993.

—————. "Seeing Suffering Directly." *Primary Point 1,* Spring 1984 www.kwanumzen.com/primarypoint/v01n2-1984-spring-jack-kornfield-seeingsufferingdirectly.html.

————— *The Wise Heart: A Guide to the Universal Teachings of Buddhist Psychology.* New York: Bantam Books, 2008.

Kornfield, Jack, and Paul Breiter, comps. *A Still Forest Pool: The Insight Meditation of Achaan Chah.* Wheaton, IL: The Theosophical Publishing House, 1985.

Matthiessen, Peter. *Nine-Headed Dragon River: Zen Journals.* Boston: Shambhala Publications, 1998.

Merton, Thomas. *The Wisdom of the Desert.* New York: New Directions, 1960.

Merzel, Dennis Genpo. *Big Mind–Big Heart: Finding Your Way.* Salt Lake City: Big Mind Publishing, 2009.

Mitchell, Stephen, ed. *Dropping Ashes on the Buddha: The Teaching of Zen Master Seung Sahn.* New York: Grove Press, 1976.

Mitchell, Stephen. *The Gospel According to Jesus: A New Translation and Guide to His Essential Teachings for Believers and Unbelievers.* New York: HarperCollins, 1991.

Moffitt, Phillip. *Dancing with Life: Buddhist Insights for Finding Meaning and Joy in the Face of Suffering.* New York: Rodale Books, 2008.

Nomura, Yushi, trans. *Desert Wisdom: Sayings from the Desert Fathers.* Maryknoll, NY: Orbis Books, 2001.

Palmer, Parker. *Let Your Life Speak: Listening for the Voice of Vocation.* San Francisco: Jossey-Bass, 2000.

Price, Reynolds. *A Whole New Life.* New York: Scribner, 2000.

Rosenberg, Marshall. *Nonviolent Communication: A Language of Life.* Encinitas, CA: PuddleDancer Press, 2005.

Shapiro, Rami. *The Divine Feminine in Biblical Wisdom Literature: Selections Annotated and Explained.* Woodstock, VT: SkyLight Paths Publishing, 2005.

—————. *Open Secrets: The Letters of Reb Yerachmiel ben Yisrael.* Rhinebeck, NY: Monkfish Publishing, 2004.

————. *The Sacred Art of Lovingkindness: Preparing to Practice.* Woodstock, VT: SkyLight Paths Publishing, 2007.

Sumedho, Ajahn. *The Mind and the Way: Buddhist Reflections on Life.* Boston: Wisdom Publications, 1996.

Szpakowski, Susan. *Speaking of Silence: Buddhists and Christians in Dialogue.* Halifax, Nova Scotia: Vajradhatu Publications, 2005.

Tarrant, John. *Bring Me the Rhinoceros: And Other Zen Koans to Bring You Joy.* New York: Harmony Books, 2004.

Trungpa, Chögyam. *Cutting Through Spiritual Materialism.* Boston: Shambhala Publications, 2002.

Tsoknyi, Rinpoche. *Carefree Dignity.* Berkeley: North Atlantic Books, 2004.

————. *Fearless Simplicity: The Dzogchen Way of Living Freely in a Complex World.* Hong Kong: Rangjung Yeshe Publications, 2003.

Walker, Alice. "Suffering Too Insignificant for the Majority to See." In *The Best Buddhist Writing 2007,* edited by Melvin McLeod. Boston: Shambhala Publications, 2007.

Welwood, John. *Perfect Love, Imperfect Relationships: Healing the Wound of the Heart.* Boston: Trumpeter Books, 2006.

Recordings

Adyashanti. *Spontaneous Awakening.* Sounds True Audio Learning Course, Session 11. Louisville, CO: Sounds True, 2005.

Websites

www.thework.com

Byron Katie's website, for more information on The Work.

www.cnvc.org

Marshall Rosenberg's website, for more information on Nonviolent Communication.

www.mlfnow.org

For more information on Mobile Loaves and Fishes.

www.insidepassages.com

Kurt Hoelting's website, for more information on Inside Passages and wilderness contemplative experiences.

Acknowledgments

There have been many benefactors in the creation of this book. Bill Parsons, Jimmy Pilkerton, and John Mogabgab all encouraged me to begin writing. John is the editor of *Weavings* and has been my spiritual friend for many blessed years. Rabbi Rami Shapiro both inspired me with his own writing and initiated me into the mysteries of getting my work published. Marcia Broucek, my editor at SkyLight Paths, helped me more than I can ever say and made this a far better book for her skillful attention and enthusiastic collaboration. A deep bow of gratitude to her.

John Johnson's affection and appreciation have encouraged me ever since we first met over twenty years ago. John died before the publication of this book, but he read and improved an early draft. John was the heart and soul of our Book Club, a group of dear friends who have cheered me on in this project. Benjamin Polansky brought his gifted writer's eye to the manuscript and made valuable suggestions. Ben Curtis is a model of the best synthesis of pastoral care and spiritual direction, and he has unfailingly given support to my writing and to what he calls my "underground ministry."

Roy Elam, Bob Smyth, Taylor Wray, Dick Bruehl, Brad Reed, Volney Gay, Cynthia Brown, Keith Meador, and David Yarian are good friends who saw me through a dark time. I wouldn't be where I am today without them. My friend Carol Elam has passed on from this life, but her bright faith is with me still. Becca Stevens welcomed me with an open heart to stand at the altar with her as a priest at St. Augustine's Episcopal Chapel at Vanderbilt. Raby Edwards, Thom Blair, Bill Sachs, Anne Stevenson, Geoffrey Butcher, and especially Tom Ward are Episcopal clergy friends who have blessed me with their companionship. Friends at St. Stephen's Episcopal Church, Richmond, Virgina, and Christ Church Cathedral, Nashville, Tennessee, showed me great kindness.

My Christian teachers, Harry Gamble, David Harned, Julian Hartt, Rowan Greer, Henri Nouwen, Geoffrey Rowthorn, John Cook, Robert Johnson, Liston Mills, Father Basil Pennington, and Father Thomas Keating, all left big footprints to follow. My Buddhist teachers, Phillip Moffitt, Tara Brach, James Baraz, Guy Armstrong, Sylvia Boorstein, and Jack Kornfield, all associated with Spirit Rock Meditation Center, embody mindfulness practice in a way that at long last has given me the feeling of being at home in the world.

Timm Glover taught me tai chi and qigong, and Sandi Anders was my first yoga teacher. These mindful movements help me wake up each day to an embodied life.

Kurt Hoelting invited me to share dharma practice in the Alaskan wilderness, and it is good karma indeed to be his friend. Bill Harkins is joining me in opening new doors for contemplative practice in the natural beauties of the Southeast. Professor John Thatamanil generously invited me to co-teach a class in Buddhist-Christian dialogue at Vanderbilt Divinity School, and I am privileged to be one of John's students.

My dharma brothers and sisters of the Spirit Rock Community Dharma Leader Training gave me an experience of what can happen when a group is committed to holding every thought and feeling in loving awareness. This book is a testament to what we learned together. My gratitude to each of them, especially Chris Cullen, Jonathan Foust, and Art Jolly.

My psychotherapy clients, mindfulness students at Vanderbilt's Center for Integrative Health and Saint Thomas

Hospital's Stress Reduction Program, and friends in the Nashville Mindfulness Meditation Group at All Faith Chapel have encouraged me as they have tested the practices in this book and shared the freedoms they have discovered.

My brother, Bill Peerman, and my friends, Rob Barrick, Berry Holt, and Alan Graham are my partners in the Mobile Loaves and Fishes ministry. These four reliably bless me with uncontrollable laughter.

My wife, Kathy, is my greatest benefactor. More than anything, this book is the fruit of our life and explorations together. My first reader and editor and partner in mindfulness teaching and practice, Kathy brings love, joy, wonder, and wisdom into my life.

My son, Alex, who brings such delight to me, lights up my life. More than anyone, this book was written for him.

> *May they all be filled with lovingkindness.*
> *May they be calm and peaceful.*
> *May they be safe and happy.*
> *May they awaken and be free.*

Credits

Grateful acknowledgment is given for permission to use material from the following sources:

Touching Peace (For more information please see Touching Peace by Thich Nhat Hanh [Berkeley, CA: Parallax Press, 1992]).

Loving What Is by Byron Katie (New York: Random House, 2003).

Emotional Alchemy by Tara Bennett-Goleman (New York: Random House, 2001).

Nonviolent Communication: A Language of Life by Marshall B. Rosenberg (Encinitas, CA: PuddleDancer Press, 2003).

The Blooming of a Lotus by Thich Nhat Hahn, Copyright © 1993 by Thich Nhat Hahn. Reprinted by permission of Beacon Press, Boston.

From Nine-Headed Dragon River, by Peter Matthiessen, © 1985 by Zen Community of New York. Reprinted by arrangement with Shambhala Publications, Inc., Boston, MA. www.shambhala.com; From Being Zen, by Ezra Bayda, © 2002 by Ezra Bayda. Reprinted by arrangement with Shambhala Publications, Inc., Boston, MA. www.shambhala.com; and "Seeing Suffering Directly" by Jack Kornfield (as printed by Primary Point Press in Primary Point, Volume 1, Spring 1984).

Grateful acknowledgment is also given to Kurt Hoelting for permission to print an account of our Alaskan trip.

Unless otherwise indicated, Scripture quotations are from the New Revised Standard Version Bible, copyright © 1989 by the Division of Christian Education of the National Council of the Churches of Christ in the USA. Used by permission. All rights reserved.

An earlier version of the Introduction appeared in Radical Grace, July/August/September 2007. Radical Grace is published by the Center for Action and Contemplation, Albuquerque, NM (www.cacradicalgrace.org/resources/radicalgrace.html).

An earlier version of the chapter "An Instrument of Peace" appeared in Weavings, March/April 1994. Weavings is published by The Upper Room, Nashville, TN (www.upperroom.org/weavings).

Inspiration

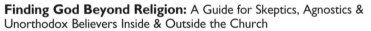

The Rebirthing of God
Christianity's Struggle for New Beginnings
By John Philip Newell
Drawing on modern prophets from East and West, and using the holy island of Iona as an icon of new beginnings, Celtic poet, peacemaker and scholar John Philip Newell dares us to imagine a new birth from deep within Christianity, a fresh stirring of the Spirit.
6 x 9, 160 pp, HC, 978-1-59473-542-4 **$19.99**

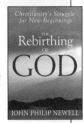

Finding God Beyond Religion: A Guide for Skeptics, Agnostics & Unorthodox Believers Inside & Outside the Church
By Tom Stella; Foreword by The Rev. Canon Marianne Wells Borg
Reinterprets traditional religious teachings central to the Christian faith for people who have outgrown the beliefs and devotional practices that once made sense to them.
6 x 9, 160 pp, Quality PB, 978-1-59473-485-4 **$16.99**

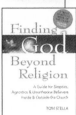

Fully Awake and Truly Alive: Spiritual Practices to Nurture Your Soul
By Rev. Jane E. Vennard; Foreword by Rami Shapiro
Illustrates the joys and frustrations of spiritual practice, offers insights from various religious traditions and provides exercises and meditations to help us become more fully alive.
6 x 9, 208 pp, Quality PB, 978-1-59473-473-1 **$16.99**

Journeys of Simplicity: Traveling Light with Thomas Merton, Bashō, Edward Abbey, Annie Dillard & Others   *By Philip Harnden*
Invites you to consider a more graceful way of traveling through life. PB includes journal pages to help you get started on your own spiritual journey.
5 x 7¼, 144 pp, Quality PB, 978-1-59473-181-5 **$12.99**
5 x 7¼, 128 pp, HC, 978-1-893361-76-8 **$16.95**

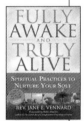

Perennial Wisdom for the Spiritually Independent
Sacred Teachings—Annotated & Explained
Annotation by Rami Shapiro; Foreword by Richard Rohr
Weaves sacred texts and teachings from the world's major religions into a coherent exploration of the five core questions at the heart of every religion's search.
5½ x 8½, 336 pp, Quality PB Original, 978-1-59473-515-8 **$16.99**

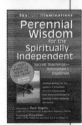

Saving Civility: 52 Ways to Tame Rude, Crude & Attitude for a Polite Planet
By Sara Hacala
Provides fifty-two practical ways you can reverse the course of incivility and make the world a more enriching, pleasant place to live.
6 x 9, 240 pp, Quality PB, 978-1-59473-314-7 **$16.99**

Spiritually Healthy Divorce: Navigating Disruption with Insight & Hope
By Carolyne Call
A spiritual map to help you move through the twists and turns of divorce.
6 x 9, 224 pp, Quality PB, 978-1-59473-288-1 **$16.99**

Or phone, fax, mail or email to: SKYLIGHT PATHS Publishing
Sunset Farm Offices, Route 4 • P.O. Box 237 • Woodstock, Vermont 05091
Tel: (802) 457-4000 • Fax: (802) 457-4004 • www.skylightpaths.com
Credit card orders: (800) 962-4544 (8:30AM–5:30PM EST Monday–Friday)
Generous discounts on quantity orders. SATISFACTION GUARANTEED. Prices subject to change.

Children's Spirituality

Adam & Eve's First Sunset: God's New Day
By Sandy Eisenberg Sasso; Full-color illus. by Joani Keller Rothenberg
A lesson in hope and faith—for every child who worries about what comes next.
9 x 12, 32 pp, Full-color illus., HC, 978-1-58023-177-0 **$17.95*** For ages 4 & up

Because Nothing Looks Like God
By Lawrence Kushner and Karen Kushner; Full-color illus. by Dawn W. Majewski
Invites parents and children to explore the questions we all have about God.
11 x 8½, 32 pp, Full-color illus., HC, 978-1-58023-092-6 **$18.99*** For ages 4 & up
Also available: **Teacher's Guide** 8½ x 11, 22 pp, PB, 978-1-58023-140-4 **$6.95**

But God Remembered: Stories of Women from Creation to the Promised Land
By Sandy Eisenberg Sasso; Full-color illus. by Bethanne Andersen
A fascinating collection of four different stories of women only briefly mentioned in biblical tradition and religious texts.
9 x 12, 32 pp, Full-color illus., Quality PB, 978-1-58023-372-9 **$8.99*** For ages 8 & up

Does God Hear My Prayer?
By August Gold; Full-color photos by Diane Hardy Waller
Introduces preschoolers and young readers to prayer and how it helps them express their own emotions.
10 x 8½, 32 pp, Full-color photo illus., Quality PB, 978-1-59473-102-0 **$8.99** For ages 3–6

For Heaven's Sake
By Sandy Eisenberg Sasso; Full-color illus. by Kathryn Kunz Finney
Heaven is often found where you least expect it.
9 x 12, 32 pp, Full-color illus., HC, 978-1-58023-054-4 **$16.95*** For ages 4 & up

God in Between
By Sandy Eisenberg Sasso; Full-color illus. by Sally Sweetland
A magical, mythical tale that teaches that God can be found where we are.
9 x 12, 32 pp, Full-color illus., HC, 978-1-879045-86-6 **$16.95*** For ages 4 & up

God's Paintbrush: Special 10th Anniversary Edition
By Sandy Eisenberg Sasso; Full-color illus. by Annette Compton
Invites children of all faiths and backgrounds to encounter God through moments in their own lives.
11 x 8½, 32 pp, Full-color illus., HC, 978-1-58023-195-4 **$17.95*** For ages 4 & up

Also available: **God's Paintbrush Teacher's Guide**
8½ x 11, 32 pp, PB, 978-1-879045-57-6 **$8.95**

God's Paintbrush Celebration Kit: A Spiritual Activity Kit for Teachers and Students of All Faiths, All Backgrounds 9½ x 12, 40 Full-color Activity Sheets & Teacher Folder w/ complete instructions, HC, 978-1-58023-050-6 **$21.95**
Additional activity sheets available:
8-Student Activity Sheet Pack (40 sheets/5 sessions), 978-1-58023-058-2 **$19.95**
Single-Student Activity Sheet Pack (5 sessions), 978-1-58023-059-9 **$3.95**

I Am God's Paintbrush (A Board Book)
By Sandy Eisenberg Sasso; Full-color illus. by Annette Compton
5 x 5, 24 pp, Full-color illus., Board Book, 978-1-59473-265-2 **$7.99** For ages 1–4

It's a ... It's a ... It's a Mitzvah
By Liz Suneby and Diane Heiman; Full-color Illus. by Laurel Molk
Introduces children through lively illustrations and playful dialogue to the everyday kindnesses that mark the beginning of a Jewish journey and a lifetime commitment to *tikkun olam* (repairing the world).
9 x 12, 32 pp Full-color illus., HC, 978-1-58023-509-9 **$18.99***

That's a Mitzvah (A Board Book)
By Liz Suneby and Diane Heiman; Full-color illus. by Laurel Molk
5 x 5, 24 pp, Full-color illus., Board Book, 978-1-58023-804-5 **$8.99*** For ages 1–4

---

*A book from Jewish Lights, SkyLight Paths' sister imprint

Prayer / Meditation

Openings, 2nd Edition
A Daybook of Saints, Sages, Psalms and Prayer Practices
By Rev. Larry J. Peacock
For anyone hungry for a richer prayer life, this prayer book offers daily inspiration to help you move closer to God. Draws on a wide variety of resources—lives of saints and sages from every age, psalms, and suggestions for personal reflection and practice.   6 x 9, 448 pp, Quality PB, 978-1-59473-545-5 **$18.99**

Men Pray: Voices of Strength, Faith, Healing, Hope and Courage
Created by the Editors at SkyLight Paths
Celebrates the rich variety of ways men around the world have called out to the Divine—with words of joy, praise, gratitude, wonder, petition and even anger—from the ancient world up to our own day.
5 x 7¼, 192 pp, HC, 978-1-59473-395-6 **$16.99**

Honest to God Prayer
Spirituality as Awareness, Empowerment, Relinquishment and Paradox
By Kent Ira Groff
For those turned off by shopworn religious language, offers innovative ways to pray based on both Native American traditions and Ignatian spirituality.
6 x 9, 192 pp, Quality PB, 978-1-59473-433-5 **$16.99**

Sacred Attention: A Spiritual Practice for Finding God in the Moment
By Margaret D. McGee
Framed on the Christian liturgical year, this inspiring guide explores ways to develop a practice of attention as a means of talking—and listening—to God.
6 x 9, 144 pp, Quality PB, 978-1-59473-291-1 **$16.99**

Praying with Our Hands: 21 Practices of Embodied Prayer from the World's
Spiritual Traditions *By Jon M. Sweeney; Photos by Jennifer J. Wilson; Foreword by Mother Tessa Bielecki; Afterword by Taitetsu Unno, PhD*
8 x 8, 96 pp, 22 duotone photos, Quality PB, 978-1-893361-16-4 **$16.95**

Secrets of Prayer: A Multifaith Guide to Creating Personal Prayer in Your Life
By Nancy Corcoran, CSJ
6 x 9, 160 pp, Quality PB, 978-1-59473-215-7 **$16.99**

Three Gates to Meditation Practice: A Personal Journey into Sufism, Buddhism,
and Judaism *By David A. Cooper* 5½ x 8½, 240 pp, Quality PB, 978-1-893361-22-5 **$18.99**

Women of Color Pray: Voices of Strength, Faith, Healing, Hope and Courage
Edited and with Introductions by Christal M. Jackson
5 x 7¼, 208 pp, Quality PB, 978-1-59473-077-1 **$15.99**

Prayer / M. Basil Pennington, OCSO

Finding Grace at the Center, 3rd Edition: The Beginning of
Centering Prayer *With Thomas Keating, OCSO, and Thomas E. Clarke, SJ; Foreword by Rev. Cynthia Bourgeault, PhD* A practical guide to a simple and beautiful form of meditative prayer. 5 x 7¼,128 pp, Quality PB, 978-1-59473-182-2 **$12.99**

The Monks of Mount Athos: A Western Monk's Extraordinary
Spiritual Journey on Eastern Holy Ground *Foreword by Archimandrite Dionysios*
Explores the landscape, monastic communities and food of Athos.
6 x 9, 352 pp, Quality PB, 978-1-893361-78-2 **$18.95**

Psalms: A Spiritual Commentary *Illus. by Phillip Ratner*
Reflections on some of the most beloved passages from the Bible's most widely read book.   6 x 9, 176 pp, 24 full-page b/w illus., Quality PB, 978-1-59473-234-8 **$16.99**

The Song of Songs: A Spiritual Commentary *Illus. by Phillip Ratner*
Explore the Bible's most challenging mystical text.
6 x 9, 160 pp, 14 full-page b/w illus., Quality PB, 978-1-59473-235-5 **$16.99**
HC, 978-1-59473-004-7 **$19.99**

Spirituality / Animal Companions

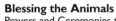

Blessing the Animals
Prayers and Ceremonies to Celebrate God's Creatures, Wild and Tame
Edited and with Introductions by Lynn L. Caruso
5 x 7¼, 256 pp, Quality PB, 978-1-59473-253-9 **$15.99**; HC, 978-1-59473-145-7 **$19.99**

Remembering My Pet
A Kid's Own Spiritual Workbook for When a Pet Dies
By Nechama Liss-Levinson, PhD, and Rev. Molly Phinney Baskette, MDiv
Foreword by Lynn L. Caruso
8 x 10, 48 pp, 2-color text, HC, 978-1-59473-221-8 **$16.99**

What Animals Can Teach Us about Spirituality
Inspiring Lessons from Wild and Tame Creatures
By Diana L. Guerrero 6 x 9, 176 pp, Quality PB, 978-1-893361-84-3 **$16.95**

Spirituality & Crafts

Beading—The Creative Spirit
Finding Your Sacred Center through the Art of Beadwork
By Rev. Wendy Ellsworth
Invites you on a spiritual pilgrimage into the kaleidoscope world of glass and color.
7 x 9, 240 pp, 8-page color insert, 40+ b/w photos and 40 diagrams, Quality PB, 978-1-59473-267-6 **$18.99**

Contemplative Crochet
A Hands-On Guide for Interlocking Faith and Craft
By Cindy Crandall-Frazier; Foreword by Linda Skolnik
Illuminates the spiritual lessons you can learn through crocheting.
7 x 9, 208 pp, b/w photos, Quality PB, 978-1-59473-238-6 **$16.99**

The Knitting Way
A Guide to Spiritual Self-Discovery
By Linda Skolnik and Janice MacDaniels
Examines how you can explore and strengthen your spiritual life through knitting.
7 x 9, 240 pp, b/w photos, Quality PB, 978-1-59473-079-5 **$16.99**

The Painting Path
Embodying Spiritual Discovery through Yoga, Brush and Color
By Linda Novick; Foreword by Richard Segalman
Explores the divine connection you can experience through art.
7 x 9, 208 pp, 8-page color insert, plus b/w photos, Quality PB, 978-1-59473-226-3 **$18.99**

The Quilting Path
A Guide to Spiritual Discovery through Fabric, Thread and Kabbalah
By Louise Silk
Explores how to cultivate personal growth through quilt making.
7 x 9, 192 pp, b/w photos and illus., Quality PB, 978-1-59473-206-5 **$16.99**

The Scrapbooking Journey
A Hands-On Guide to Spiritual Discovery
By Cory Richardson-Lauve; Foreword by Stacy Julian
Reveals how this craft can become a practice used to deepen and shape your life.
7 x 9, 176 pp, 8-page color insert, plus b/w photos, Quality PB, 978-1-59473-216-4 **$18.99**

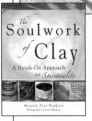

The Soulwork of Clay
A Hands-On Approach to Spirituality
By Marjory Zoet Bankson; Photos by Peter Bankson
Takes you through the seven-step process of making clay into a pot, drawing parallels at each stage to the process of spiritual growth.
7 x 9, 192 pp, b/w photos, Quality PB, 978-1-59473-249-2 **$16.99**

Spirituality

Like a Child
Restoring the Awe, Wonder, Joy and Resiliency of the Human Spirit
By Rev. Timothy J. Mooney
By breaking free from our misperceptions about what it means to be an adult, we can reshape our world and become harbingers of grace. This unique spiritual resource explores Jesus's counsel to become like children in order to enter the kingdom of God.   6 x 9, 160 pp, Quality PB, 978-1-59473-543-1 **$16.99**

The Passionate Jesus: What We Can Learn from Jesus about Love, Fear, Grief, Joy and Living Authentically
By The Rev. Peter Wallace
Reveals Jesus as a passionate figure who was involved, present, connected, honest and direct with others and encourages you to build personal authenticity in every area of your own life. 6 x 9, 208 pp, Quality PB, 978-1-59473-393-2 **$18.99**

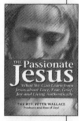

Gathering at God's Table: The Meaning of Mission in the Feast of Faith
By Katharine Jefferts Schori
A profound reminder of our role in the larger frame of God's dream for a restored and reconciled world.   6 x 9, 256 pp, HC, 978-1-59473-316-1 **$21.99**

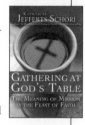

The Heartbeat of God: Finding the Sacred in the Middle of Everything
By Katharine Jefferts Schori; Foreword by Joan Chittister, OSB
Explores our connections to other people, to other nations and with the environment through the lens of faith.
6 x 9, 240 pp, HC, 978-1-59473-292-8 **$21.99**

A Dangerous Dozen: Twelve Christians Who Threatened the Status Quo but Taught Us to Live Like Jesus
By the Rev. Canon C. K. Robertson, PhD; Foreword by Archbishop Desmond Tutu
Profiles twelve visionary men and women who challenged society and showed the world a different way of living.
6 x 9, 208 pp, Quality PB, 978-1-59473-298-0 **$16.99**

Laugh Your Way to Grace: Reclaiming the Spiritual Power of Humor
By Rev. Susan Sparks
A powerful, humorous case for laughter as a spiritual, healing path.
6 x 9, 176 pp, Quality PB, 978-1-59473-280-5 **$16.99**

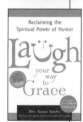

Claiming Earth as Common Ground: The Ecological Crisis through the Lens of Faith
By Andrea Cohen-Kiener; Foreword by Rev. Sally Bingham
6 x 9, 192 pp, Quality PB, 978-1-59473-261-4 **$16.99**

Living into Hope: A Call to Spiritual Action for Such a Time as This
By Rev. Dr. Joan Brown Campbell; Foreword by Karen Armstrong
6 x 9, 208 pp, Quality PB, 978-1-59473-436-6 $18.99; HC, 978-1-59473-283-6 **$21.99**

Renewal in the Wilderness
A Spiritual Guide to Connecting with God in the Natural World
By John Lionberger 6 x 9, 176 pp, b/w photos, Quality PB, 978-1-59473-219-5 **$16.99**

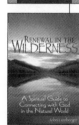

Spiritual Adventures in the Snow
Skiing & Snowboarding as Renewal for Your Soul
By Dr. Marcia McFee and Rev. Karen Foster; Foreword by Paul Arthur
5½ x 8½, 208 pp, Quality PB, 978-1-59473-270-6 **$16.99**

A Walk with Four Spiritual Guides: Krishna, Buddha, Jesus, and Ramakrishna
By Andrew Harvey 5½ x 8½ 192 pp, b/w photos & illus., Quality PB, 978-1-59473-138-9 **$15.99**

Who Is My God? 2nd Edition: An Innovative Guide to Finding Your Spiritual Identity
By the Editors at SkyLight Paths
Provides the Spiritual Identity Self-Test™ to uncover the components of your unique spirituality.
6 x 9, 160 pp, Quality PB, 978-1-59473-014-6 **$15.99**

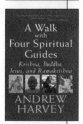

Retirement and Later-Life Spirituality

Caresharing
A Reciprocal Approach to Caregiving and Care Receiving in the Complexities of Aging, Illness or Disability
By Marty Richards
Shows how to move from independent to *inter*dependent caregiving, so that the "cared for" and the "carer" share a deep sense of connection.
6 x 9, 256 pp, Quality PB, 978-1-59473-286-7 **$16.99**; HC, 978-1-59473-247-8 **$24.99**

How Did I Get to Be 70 When I'm 35 Inside?
Spiritual Surprises of Later Life
By Linda Douty
Encourages you to focus on the inner changes of aging to help you greet your later years as the grand adventure they can be.
6 x 9, 208 pp, Quality PB, 978-1-59473-297-3 **$16.99**

Soul Fire
Accessing Your Creativity
By Thomas Ryan, CSP
This inspiring guide shows you how to cultivate your creative spirit, particularly in the second half of life, as a way to encourage personal growth, enrich your spiritual life and deepen your communion with God.
6 x 9, 160 pp, Quality PB, 978-1-59473-243-0 **$16.99**

Restoring Life's Missing Pieces
The Spiritual Power of Remembering & Reuniting with People, Places, Things & Self
By Caren Goldman; Foreword by Dr. Nancy Copeland-Payton
Delve deeply into ways that your body, mind and spirit answer the Spirit of Re-union's calls to reconnect with people, places, things and self. A powerful and thought-provoking look at "reunions" of all kinds as roads to remembering the missing pieces of our stories, psyches and souls.
6 x 9, 208 pp, Quality PB, 978-1-59473-295-9 **$16.99**

Creative Aging
Rethinking Retirement and Non-Retirement in a Changing World
By Marjory Zoet Bankson
Explores the spiritual dimensions of retirement and aging and offers creative ways for you to share your gifts and experience, particularly when retirement leaves you questioning who you are when you are no longer defined by your career.
6 x 9, 160 pp, Quality PB, 978-1-59473-281-2 **$16.99**

Creating a Spiritual Retirement
A Guide to the Unseen Possibilities in Our Lives
By Molly Srode
Retirement can be an opportunity to refocus on your soul and deepen the presence of spirit in your life. With fresh spiritual reflections and questions to help you explore this new phase.
6 x 9, 208 pp, b/w photos, Quality PB, 978-1-59473-050-4 **$14.99**

Keeping Spiritual Balance as We Grow Older
More than 65 Creative Ways to Use Purpose, Prayer, and the Power of Spirit to Build a Meaningful Retirement
By Molly and Bernie Srode
As we face new demands on our bodies, it's easy to focus on the physical and forget about the transformations in our spiritual selves. This book is brimming with creative, practical ideas to add purpose and spirit to a meaningful retirement.
8 x 8, 224 pp, Quality PB, 978-1-59473-042-9 **$16.99**

Spiritual Practice—The Sacred Art of Living Series

Dreaming—The Sacred Art: Incubating, Navigating & Interpreting Sacred Dreams for Spiritual & Personal Growth
By Lori Joan Swick
This fascinating introduction to sacred dreams celebrates the dream experience as a way to deepen spiritual awareness and as a source of self-healing. Designed for the novice and the experienced sacred dreamer of all faith traditions, or none.
5½ x 8½, 224 pp, Quality PB, 978-1-59473-544-8 **$16.99**

Conversation—The Sacred Art: Practicing Presence in an Age of Distraction
By Diane M. Millis, PhD; Foreword by Rev. Tilden Edwards, PhD
5½ x 8½, 192 pp, Quality PB, 978-1-59473-474-8 **$16.99**

Dance—The Sacred Art: The Joy of Movement as a Spiritual Practice
By Cynthia Winton-Henry 5½ x 8½, 224 pp, Quality PB, 978-1-59473-268-3 **$16.99**

Fly-Fishing—The Sacred Art: Casting a Fly as a Spiritual Practice
By Rabbi Eric Eisenkramer and Rev. Michael Attas, MD; Foreword by Chris Wood, CEO, Trout Unlimited; Preface by Lori Simon, executive director, Casting for Recovery
5½ x 8½, 160 pp, Quality PB, 978-1-59473-299-7 **$16.99**

Giving—The Sacred Art: Creating a Lifestyle of Generosity
By Lauren Tyler Wright 5½ x 8½, 208 pp, Quality PB, 978-1-59473-224-9 **$16.99**

Haiku—The Sacred Art: A Spiritual Practice in Three Lines
By Margaret D. McGee 5½ x 8½, 192 pp, Quality PB, 978-1-59473-269-0 **$16.99**

Hospitality—The Sacred Art: Discovering the Hidden Spiritual Power of Invitation and Welcome *By Rev. Nanette Sawyer; Foreword by Rev. Dirk Ficca*
5½ x 8½, 208 pp, Quality PB, 978-1-59473-228-7 **$16.99**

Labyrinths from the Outside In, 2nd Edition: Walking to Spiritual Insight—A Beginner's Guide *By Rev. Dr. Donna Schaper and Rev. Dr. Carole Ann Camp*
6 x 9, 208 pp, b/w illus. and photos, Quality PB, 978-1-59473-486-1 **$16.99**

Lectio Divina—**The Sacred Art**
Transforming Words & Images into Heart-Centered Prayer
By Christine Valters Paintner, PhD 5½ x 8½, 240 pp, Quality PB, 978-1-59473-300-0 **$16.99**

Pilgrimage—The Sacred Art: Journey to the Center of the Heart
By Dr. Sheryl A. Kujawa-Holbrook 5½ x 8½, 240 pp, Quality PB, 978-1-59473-472-4 **$16.99**

Practicing the Sacred Art of Listening: A Guide to Enrich Your Relationships and Kindle Your Spiritual Life *By Kay Lindahl* 8 x 8, 176 pp, Quality PB, 978-1-893361-85-0 **$18.99**

Recovery—The Sacred Art: The Twelve Steps as Spiritual Practice *by Rami Shapiro; Foreword by Joan Borysenko, PhD* 5½ x 8½, 240 pp, Quality PB, 978-1-59473-259-1 **$16.99**

Running—The Sacred Art: Preparing to Practice *By Dr. Warren A. Kay; Foreword by Kristin Armstrong* 5½ x 8½, 160 pp, Quality PB, 978-1-59473-227-0 **$16.99**

The Sacred Art of Chant: Preparing to Practice
By Ana Hernández 5½ x 8½, 192 pp, Quality PB, 978-1-59473-036-8 **$16.99**

The Sacred Art of Fasting: Preparing to Practice
By Thomas Ryan, CSP 5½ x 8½, 192 pp, Quality PB, 978-1-59473-078-8 **$15.99**

The Sacred Art of Forgiveness: Forgiving Ourselves and Others through God's Grace
By Marcia Ford 8 x 8, 176 pp, Quality PB, 978-1-59473-175-4 **$18.99**

The Sacred Art of Listening: Forty Reflections for Cultivating a Spiritual Practice
By Kay Lindahl; Illus. by Amy Schnapper 8 x 8, 160 pp, b/w illus., Quality PB, 978-1-893361-44-7 **$16.99**

The Sacred Art of Lovingkindness: Preparing to Practice
By Rabbi Rami Shapiro; Foreword by Marcia Ford 5½ x 8½, 176 pp, Quality PB, 978-1-59473-151-8 **$16.99**

Thanking & Blessing—The Sacred Art: Spiritual Vitality through Gratefulness
By Jay Marshall, PhD; Foreword by Philip Gulley 5½ x 8½, 176 pp, Quality PB, 978-1-59473-231-7 **$16.99**

Writing—The Sacred Art: Beyond the Page to Spiritual Practice
By Rami Shapiro and Aaron Shapiro 5½ x 8½, 192 pp, Quality PB, 978-1-59473-372-7 **$16.99**

Women's Interest

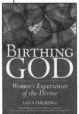

Birthing God: Women's Experiences of the Divine
By Lana Dalberg; Foreword by Kathe Schaaf
Powerful narratives of suffering, love and hope that inspire both personal and collective transformation. 6 x 9, 304 pp, Quality PB, 978-1-59473-480-9 **$18.99**

On the Chocolate Trail: A Delicious Adventure Connecting Jews, Religions, History, Travel, Rituals and Recipes to the Magic of Cacao
By Rabbi Deborah R. Prinz
Take a delectable journey through the religious history of chocolate—a real treat!
6 x 9, 272 pp, 20+ b/w photographs, Quality PB, 978-1-58023-487-0 **$18.99***

Women, Spirituality and Transformative Leadership
Where Grace Meets Power
Edited by Kathe Schaaf, Kay Lindahl, Kathleen S. Hurty, PhD, and Reverend Guo Cheen
A dynamic conversation on the power of women's spiritual leadership and its emerging patterns of transformation.
6 x 9, 288 pp, Quality PB, 978-1-59473-548-6 **$18.99**; HC, 978-1-59473-313-0 **$24.99**

Spiritually Healthy Divorce: Navigating Disruption with Insight & Hope
By Carolyne Call A spiritual map to help you move through the twists and turns of divorce. 6 x 9, 224 pp, Quality PB, 978-1-59473-288-1 **$16.99**

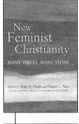

New Feminist Christianity: Many Voices, Many Views
Edited by Mary E. Hunt and Diann L. Neu
Insights from ministers and theologians, activists and leaders, artists and liturgists offer a starting point for building new models of religious life and worship.
6 x 9, 384 pp, Quality PB, 978-1-59473-435-9 **$19.99**; HC, 978-1-59473-285-0 **$24.99**

Bread, Body, Spirit: Finding the Sacred in Food
Edited and with Introductions by Alice Peck 6 x 9, 224 pp, Quality PB, 978-1-59473-242-3 **$19.99**

Dance—The Sacred Art: The Joy of Movement as a Spiritual Practice
By Cynthia Winton-Henry 5½ x 8½, 224 pp, Quality PB, 978-1-59473-268-3 **$16.99**

Daughters of the Desert: Stories of Remarkable Women from Christian, Jewish and Muslim Traditions
By Claire Rudolf Murphy, Meghan Nuttall Sayres, Mary Cronk Farrell, Sarah Conover and Betsy Wharton
5½ x 8½, 192 pp, Illus., Quality PB, 978-1-59473-106-8 **$14.99** Inc. reader's discussion guide

The Divine Feminine in Biblical Wisdom Literature
Selections Annotated & Explained
Translation & Annotation by Rabbi Rami Shapiro; Foreword by Rev. Cynthia Bourgeault, PhD
5½ x 8½, 240 pp, Quality PB, 978-1-59473-109-9 **$16.99**

Divining the Body: Reclaim the Holiness of Your Physical Self
By Jan Phillips 8 x 8, 256 pp, Quality PB, 978-1-59473-080-1 **$18.99**

Honoring Motherhood: Prayers, Ceremonies & Blessings
Edited and with Introductions by Lynn L. Caruso
5 x 7¼, 272 pp, Quality PB, 978-1-58473-384-0 **$9.99**; HC, 978-1-59473-239-3 **$19.99**

Next to Godliness: Finding the Sacred in Housekeeping
Edited by Alice Peck 6 x 9, 224 pp, Quality PB, 978-1-59473-214-0 **$19.99**

ReVisions: Seeing Torah through a Feminist Lens
By Rabbi Elyse Goldstein 5½ x 8½, 224 pp, Quality PB, 978-1-58023-117-6 **$16.95***

The Triumph of Eve & Other Subversive Bible Tales
By Matt Biers-Ariel 5½ x 8½, 192 pp, Quality PB, 978-1-59473-176-1 **$14.99**

White Fire: A Portrait of Women Spiritual Leaders in America
By Malka Drucker; Photos by Gay Block 7 x 10, 320 pp, b/w photos, HC, 978-1-893361-64-5 **$24.95**

Woman Spirit Awakening in Nature: Growing Into the Fullness of Who You Are
By Nancy Barrett Chickerneo, PhD; Foreword by Eileen Fisher
8 x 8, 224 pp, b/w illus., Quality PB, 978-1-59473-250-8 **$16.99**

Women of Color Pray: Voices of Strength, Faith, Healing, Hope and Courage
Edited and with Introductions by Christal M. Jackson
5 x 7¼, 208 pp, Quality PB, 978-1-59473-077-1 **$15.99**

* A book from Jewish Lights, SkyLight Paths' sister imprint

Personal Growth

Decision Making & Spiritual Discernment
The Sacred Art of Finding Your Way
By Nancy L. Bieber

Presents three essential aspects of Spirit-led decision making: willingness, attentiveness and responsiveness.

5½ x 8½, 208 pp, Quality PB, 978-1-59473-289-8 **$16.99**

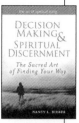

Like a Child
Restoring the Awe, Wonder, Joy and Resiliency of the Human Spirit
By Rev. Timothy J. Mooney

By breaking free from our misperceptions about what it means to be an adult, we can reshape our world and become harbingers of grace. This unique spiritual resource explores Jesus's counsel to become like children in order to enter the kingdom of God.

6 x 9, 160 pp, Quality PB, 978-1-59473-543-1 **$16.99**

Secrets of a Soulful Marriage
Creating & Sustaining a Loving, Sacred Relationship
By Jim Sharon, EdD, and Ruth Sharon, MS

An innovative, hope-filled resource for developing soulful, mature love for committed couples who are looking to create, maintain and glorify the sacred in their relationship. Offers a banquet of practical tools, inspirational real-life stories and spiritual practices for couples of all faiths, or none.

6 x 9, 200 pp (est), Quality PB, 978-1-59473-554-7 **$16.99**

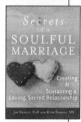

Conversation—The Sacred Art
Practicing Presence in an Age of Distraction
By Diane M. Millis, PhD; Foreword by Rev. Tilden Edwards, PhD

Cultivate the potential for deeper connection in every conversation.

5½ x 8½, 192 pp, Quality PB, 978-1-59473-474-8 **$16.99**

Hospitality—The Sacred Art
Discovering the Hidden Spiritual Power of Invitation and Welcome
By Rev. Nanette Sawyer; Foreword by Rev. Dirk Ficca

Discover how the qualities of hospitality can deepen your self-understanding and help you build transforming and lasting relationships with others and with God.

5½ x 8½, 208 pp, Quality PB, 978-1-59473-228-7 **$16.99**

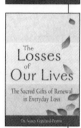

The Losses of Our Lives
The Sacred Gifts of Renewal in Everyday Loss
By Dr. Nancy Copeland-Payton

Shows us that by becoming aware of what our lesser losses have to teach us, the larger losses become less terrifying. Includes spiritual practices and questions for reflection.

6 x 9, 192 pp, Quality PB, 978-1-59473-307-9 **$16.99**; HC, 978-1-59473-271-3 **$19.99**

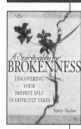

A Spirituality for Brokenness
Discovering Your Deepest Self in Difficult Times
By Terry Taylor

Compassionately guides you through the practicalities of facing and finally accepting brokenness in your life—a process that can ultimately bring mending.

6 x 9, 176 pp, Quality PB, 978-1-59473-229-4 **$16.99**

The Bridge to Forgiveness
Stories and Prayers for Finding God and Restoring Wholeness
By Karyn D. Kedar

This inspiring guide for healing and wholeness supplies you with a map to help you along your forgiveness journey. Deeply personal stories, comforting prayers and intimate meditations gently lead you through the steps that allow the heart to forgive.

6 x 9, 176 pp, Quality PB, 978-1-58023-451-1 **$16.99***

* A book from Jewish Lights, SkyLight Paths' sister imprint

About SKYLIGHT PATHS Publishing

SkyLight Paths Publishing is creating a place where people of different spiritual traditions come together for challenge and inspiration, a place where we can help each other understand the mystery that lies at the heart of our existence.

Through spirituality, our religious beliefs are increasingly becoming a part of our lives—rather than *apart* from our lives. While many of us may be more interested than ever in spiritual growth, we may be less firmly planted in traditional religion. Yet, we do want to deepen our relationship to the sacred, to learn from our own as well as from other faith traditions, and to practice in new ways.

SkyLight Paths sees both believers and seekers as a community that increasingly transcends traditional boundaries of religion and denomination—people wanting to learn from each other, *walking together, finding the way.*

For your information and convenience, at the back of this book we have provided a list of other SkyLight Paths books you might find interesting and useful. They cover the following subjects:

Buddhism / Zen	Gnosticism	Poetry
Catholicism	Hinduism /	Prayer
Chaplaincy	Vedanta	Religious Etiquette
Children's Books	Inspiration	Retirement & Later-
Christianity	Islam / Sufism	Life Spirituality
Comparative	Judaism	Spiritual Biography
Religion	Meditation	Spiritual Direction
Earth-Based	Mindfulness	Spirituality
Spirituality	Monasticism	Women's Interest
Enneagram	Mysticism	Worship
Global Spiritual	Personal Growth	
Perspectives		

Or phone, fax, mail or email to: SKYLIGHT PATHS Publishing
Sunset Farm Offices, Route 4 • P.O. Box 237 • Woodstock, Vermont 05091
Tel: (802) 457-4000 • Fax: (802) 457-4004 • www.skylightpaths.com
Credit card orders: (800) 962-4544 (8:30AM–5:30PM EST Monday–Friday)
Generous discounts on quantity orders. SATISFACTION GUARANTEED. Prices subject to change.